CW00421189

# Chinese Macbeth
# PLAYbook

Annabelle Howard

This book is dedicated to
children, teachers, and parents
everywhere.

# CONTENTS

# ACKNOWLEDGMENTS

This book was supported by a grant from the Dudley T. Doughtery Foundation in Texas, USA. The development of the script and teaching activities happened at The Barnard School in New York City. Additional work took place at The O'Neill Center in Waterford, Connecticut.

# 1 ADAPTATION

## CAST OF CHARACTERS

(in order of appearance)

**WITCHES 1-3** . . . supernatural sisters

**SOLDIER** . . . a badly wounded Scottish soldier

**KING DUNCAN** . . . King of Scotland

**ROSSE** {ROHS} . . . a Scottish nobleman

**LENNOX** . . . a Scottish nobleman

**MACBETH** {mehk-BETH} . . . a Scottish general

**BANQUO** {BAN-kwoe} . . . a Scottish general

**LADY MACBETH** . . . Macbeth's wife

**PORTER** . . . a guard at Macbeth's castle

**MACDUFF** {mehk-DUFF} . . . a Scottish nobleman

**MALCOLM** . . . King Duncan's son

**DONALBAIN** {DOHN-ehl-bane} . . . King Duncan's son

**MURDERERS 1 and 2** . . . hired thugs

**ANGUS** . . . a Scottish nobleman

**MENTEITH** {MEN-teeth} . . . a Scottish nobleman

**GHOST OF BANQUO** . . . a spirit that haunts Macbeth

**WINE SERVER** . . . a servant at Macbeth's castle

**DOCTOR** . . . a doctor in Macbeth's service

**LADY-IN-WAITING** . . . Lady Macbeth's personal servant

**MESSENGER** . . . a messenger in Macbeth's service

**SEYTON** {SEE-tehn} . . . an officer in Macbeth's army

**SIWARD** {SIGH-wehrd} . . . general of the English army

**LORDS 4-8** . . . Lords in Malcolm's service

1

| | ENGLISH | CHINESE (Simplified) |
|---|---|---|
| ACT 1, Scene 1 | | |
| (The place is a field in Scotland. Three witches enter, running. They join hands and circle very fast while counting to ten silently. At ten, they stop. They are weird!) | | |
| WITCH 1 | You, you, and me; we three, let's see . . . | 你、你、还有我自己，让我们来看看。．． |
| WITCH 2 | We'll do this again. | 我们一定会再相聚。 |
| WITCH 3 | But when? In thunder, lightning, or rain? | 但是在什么时候？在雷电或雨中相聚？ |
| WITCH 1 | When the hurlyburly's over. | 等这场喧嚣结束了。 |
| WITCH 2 | When they've got what they want and lost it. | 等他们已经得到了他们想要的并失去的时候。 |
| WITCH 3 | Tonight. | 就在今夜。 |
| WITCH 1 | In the woods. | 在树林里。 |
| WITCH 2 | And there we'll meet Macbeth. | 在那儿我们会遇见Macbeth。 |
| ALL THREE WITCHES | Good looks bad, and bad looks good. | 好事看上去也有些糟，而坏事似乎也不赖。 |
| WITCH 3 | Let's move and go. | 让我们动身去吧。 |
| WITCH 1 | And wait. | 等待着。 |
| WITCH 2 | And watch. | 观察着。 |
| (They exit suddenly, running.) | | |
| ⏎ | | |

| ACT 1, Scene 2 | | |
|---|---|---|
| (A badly wounded soldier enters first. Then King Duncan of Scotland enters, followed by Rosse and Lennox. They are close to the battlefield.) | | |

| | | |
|---|---|---|
| KING DUNCAN | I can see that you are hurt badly by the fighting, soldier, but can you report how we are doing against the rebellious Macdonwald. Speak! | 我能看出你因为战争受的重伤，我的士兵，但你可以汇报我们是如何对抗那反叛的Macdonwald吗？快说！ |
| SOLDIER | Your generals are doing a great job out there, King Duncan. Macbeth has killed that upstart Macdonwald. Macbeth has stuck Macdonwald's head on the end of a pole to encourage his own men. | Duncan国王，您的将军正在那儿进行着壮举。Macbeth已经杀了那个傲慢无礼的Macdonwald。Macbeth将Macdonwald的头颅挑在了杆子的末端来激励他的士兵。 |
| KING DUNCAN | Macbeth is a brave man. | Macbeth是位勇敢的人。 |
| SOLDIER | Your thane of Cawdor is another story. He has helped the enemy. But Macbeth and Banquo have already made the traitor suffer. | 而您的Cawdor的伯爵则不然。他帮助了敌人。但Macbeth和Banquo早已使叛徒遭受了痛苦。 |
| KING DUNCAN | The Thane of Cawdor is a traitor, and I will see that he dies because of it. Macbeth will be the new Thane of Cawdor. Macbeth deserves the honor. | Cawdor的伯爵是个叛徒，并且我会看到他因叛变而死亡。Macbeth会成为Cawdor的新伯爵。这是Macbeth应得的荣誉。 |
| (They exit.)☒ | | |
| ACT 1, Scene 3 | | |
| (The three witches enter a wild part of | | |

| | | |
|---|---|---|
| the woods.) | | |
| WITCH 1 | Where have you been? | 你去哪里了？ |
| WITCH 2 | Meddling. | 不要多管闲事。 |
| WITCH 3 | And you? | 你呢？ |
| WITCH 1 | About. Sailing in a boat full of holes. Running like a rat without a tail. | 闲逛。驾驶着千疮百孔的船航行，就像无尾之鼠在奔跑。 |
| WITCH 2 | Look at this! | 看看这个！ |
| WITCH 3 | A man's thumb! | 人的拇指！ |
| ALL THREE WITCHES | Mmmmmm! | 呒！ |
| WITCH 1 | Shh! Here comes Macbeth! | 嘘！Macbeth来了！ |
| (Macbeth and Banquo enter.) | | |
| MACBETH | We've had a good day. But this fog is bad. | 我们度过了美好的一天，但这雾有些糟。 |
| (Banquo sees the witches.) | | |
| BANQUO | What the . . . Are you dead or alive? | 欧我的天.... 你是活着还是死了？ |
| WITCH 1 | Welcome, Macbeth, thane of Glamis! | 欢迎您，Macbeth，Glamis的伯爵！ |
| WITCH 2 | Welcome, Macbeth, thane of Cawdor! | 欢迎您，Macbeth，Cawdor的伯爵！ |
| WITCH 3 | Welcome, Macbeth, soon to be called king! | 欢迎您，Macbeth，即将登基的国王！ |
| MACBETH | No! | 不！ |
| BANQUO | What's wrong? "King." Sounds good to me. | 怎么了？"国王"。听起来很适合我。 |
| WITCH 1 | Welcome! | 欢迎！ |
| WITCH 2 | Welcome! | 欢迎！ |

| | | |
|---|---|---|
| WITCH 3 | Welcome! | 欢迎！ |
| WITCH 1<br>(To Banquo) | Less than Macbeth, but more. | 比 Macbeth小些，可又大些。 |
| WITCH 2 | Not as happy, but so much happier. | 没有他那么幸福，可是又比他幸福些。 |
| WITCH 3 | Not king, but father of kings. | 虽然你不能为王，但却是多个国王的父亲。 |
| (The witches disappear.) | | |
| MACBETH | Come back here! What do you mean? The Thane of Cawdor and King Duncan are still alive! | 给我回来！你们这是什么意思？Cawdor的伯爵和Duncan国王都还活着！ |
| BANQUO | There are some weird things in this world, and we just saw three of them. | 这世界上有许多怪异的事儿，我们只是看到了其中的三件。 |
| MACBETH | They just said your children would be kings. | 他们只是说你的孩子将成为国王。 |
| BANQUO | And you'd be Thane of Cawdor and then king. Who's there? | 还有你将成为Cawdor的伯爵，然后成为国王。谁在那儿？ |
| (Rosse enters.) | | |

| | | |
|---|---|---|
| ROSSE | I am Rosse, a Scottish nobleman. I've been sent from the King to tell you that the traitor once known as the Thane of Cawdor is dead. You, Macbeth, have been named the new Thane of Cawdor. | 我是Rosse，是苏格兰贵族。国王派我来告诉你，那个一度被称为Cawdor的伯爵的叛徒已经死了。而你Macbeth，将成为Cawdor的新伯爵。 |
| (Rosse exits.) | | |
| MACBETH | Maybe your children will be kings. | 也许你的孩子将成为国王。 |
| BANQUO | It was a coincidence, Macbeth. Forget those evil creatures, or you'll regret it. I'll see you in King Duncan's palace. | 这是个巧合，Macbeth。忘记那些邪恶的生物，否则你会后悔的。我会在Duncan国王的宫殿里见你。 |
| (Banquo exits.) | | |
| MACBETH (Macbeth thinks aloud.) | Are these supernatural creatures evil or good? They told me good news, but they scare me. Maybe I will be made king, just as I was made Thane of Cawdor. I must talk to Lady Macbeth. | 那些超自然的生物是恶意还是善意？他们告诉了我好消息，但也吓唬了我。也许我会成为国王，就像我做了Cawdor的伯爵一样。我必须和Macbeth夫人谈谈。 |
| (Macbeth exits.) | | |
| ⏺ | | |
| ACT 1, Scene 4 | | |
| (Macbeth's castle in Inverness, Scotland. Lady Macbeth enters, reading a letter from Macbeth.) | | |

| LADY MACBETH | I saw the witches the day I was made Thane of Cawdor. They predicted my new title. They also said I'd be called king. I knew this would make you happy, and I couldn't wait to tell you. I am on my way to you now, and King Duncan is following close behind me. Prepare the castle for our important visitor. | 在我成为Cawdor的伯爵那天我遇见了那些女巫。她们预测了我的新头衔，并且说我将被称王。我知道这会令你开心，就迫不及待地告诉了你。我现在正在到你那里的路上，并且Duncan国王就跟在我身后不远处。布置城堡准备迎接我们重要的来宾。 |
|---|---|---|
| (Now, Lady Macbeth thinks aloud.) | | |
| | We must make our move now, Macbeth, but you worry me. You want to be great, and you're ambitious, but you just aren't quite evil enough to do what it takes to become king. I shall have to forget that I'm a woman for a while. I must be strong enough for two; otherwise, Macbeth will never be king. I must be cruel. | 我们现在必须行动起来，Macbeth，但我知道你担心我。你有想成为伟大的人，并且雄心勃勃，但要想成为国王你的邪恶还不足够。我应该不得不暂时忘记我是个女人的身份，我必须变得像两个人那样强大。否则Macbeth永远都成不了王。我必须是残酷的。 |
| (Macbeth enters.) | | |
| | Welcome, my dear and honored husband. Things are working out well for us. | 欢迎您，我尊敬又亲爱的丈夫。事情正向对我们有利的方向进展。 |

8

| MACBETH | Yes, but there is bad news. Malcolm has been made Prince of Cumberland. That means Malcolm will be the next King of Scotland – unless I stop him. | 是的，但也有坏消息。Malcolm已经成为了Cumberland的王子。这意味着Malcolm会成为苏格兰的下一任国王 – 除非我阻止他。 |
|---|---|---|
| LADY MACBETH | When is King Duncan leaving our castle? | Duncan国王何时离开我们的城堡？ |
| MACBETH | Tomorrow. | 明天。 |
| LADY MACBETH | That's what he thinks. Prepare for our regal visitor. Look happy. | 这是他所想的。准备迎接我们的皇室来宾。要面露喜色。 |

| MACBETH | We'll have to talk about this some more. | 关于这事我们要再谈谈。 |
|---|---|---|
| LADY MACBETH | I'll take care of this. But, for goodness' sake, look happy. | 我会搞定这件事。但看在上帝的面上，要面露喜色。 |
| (They exit.) | | |
| ⏷ | | |
| ACT 1, Scene 5 | | |
| (Inverness, King Duncan, Rosse, Banquo, and Lennox enter the grounds of Macbeth's castle.) | | |
| KING DUNCAN | This castle was built in a beautiful place. | 这座城堡建在了一个美丽的地方。 |
| BANQUO | It's so peaceful here. | 这里如此地宁静。 |
| (Lady Macbeth enters.) | | |
| KING DUNCAN | Our good hostess! Give me your hand, good lady, and lead us to our noble host, the Thane of Cawdor. | 我们尊贵的女主人！把手给我，尊贵的夫人，带我们去见我们的尊贵的主人 - Cawdor的伯爵。 |
| (They exit.) | | |
| ⏷ | | |
| ACT 1, Scene 6 | | |
| (Inverness. Macbeth enters a room leading off the dining room.) | | |
| MACBETH | If I'm going to do it, I'd better get it over with quickly. But I am his cousin, I am his honored subject, and I am his host. Duncan trusts me. He's such a gentle and an honest king. The only thing | 如果我要去做这事，那最好是快点结束它。可我是他的表弟，是他引以为傲的主题，并且是他的主人。Duncan 信任我，他是如此温柔和诚实的国王 |

| | that makes me want to kill Duncan is my ambition. | 。唯一让我想杀死Duncan的是我的雄心。 |
| --- | --- | --- |
| (Lady Macbeth enters.) | | |
| LADY MACBETH | What are you doing out here? | 你在那里干什么？ |
| MACBETH | I can't see this thing through. He's been too good to me. | 我无法看透这件事情。他一直对我太好了。 |
| LADY MACBETH | Do you want to live the rest of your life saying, "I might have been king. I could have been king if I'd dared to be"? | 你希望你的后半生在不断地对自己说"我本来可能是国王。如果我敢那么做，我本来应该是国王"中度过吗？ |
| MACBETH | Shut up, woman! I can only do what a man can do. If I did more, I'd be a monster. | 闭嘴吧女人！适合男子汉的行为我都敢去做。可如果我做多了，我将变成怪物。 |
| LADY MACBETH | Were you not a man when you promised you would do this? Now that Duncan is here, what are you? If I made this promise to you, I would do it, no matter what. | 当你承诺你会这么做的时候你就不是男子汉了吗？既然Duncan在这儿，那么你算什么呢？如果我向你许下诺言，无论如何我都会去做。 |
| MACBETH | But what if something goes wrong? | 但如果有些事出错了呢？ |
| LADY MACBETH | It won't. I'll put something in the guards' drinks that will make them sleep. Then you can stab Duncan with the | 不会的。我在守卫的酒里放了些东西会使他们人睡，然后你可以拿着守卫的短剑刺死Duncan |

11

| | | |
|---|---|---|
| | guards' own daggers, and in the morning, it'll look like the guards did it. | 。到了第二天早上，这一切看上去就像是守卫做的一样。 |
| MACBETH | OK. I'll do it. Let's get back to him now. The fake expressions on our faces must hide the real feelings and plans we have. | 好的，我会这么做。现在让我们回到他身边吧。我们内心真实的感受和计划必须隐藏在脸上虚伪表情的后面。 |
| (They exit.) | | |
| ⏰ | | |

| | | |
|---|---|---|
| ACT 2, Scene 1 | | |
| (Inverness. Macbeth enters the hallway outside King Duncan's bedroom.) | | |
| MACBETH (Macbeth thinks aloud.) | Am I imagining things? I could swear there is a dagger right there in front of me, pointing the way to Duncan's bedroom. A dagger just as real as this one. (He feels his own dagger.) And now it looks bloodstained! It's so dark tonight that the whole world seems strangely dead. The wolves are howling. It's as if I could feel evil all around me. But I'm wasting precious time here. | 我是在幻想着什么吗？我可以发誓有一把短剑就放在我的面前，指着那条通往Duncan卧室的路。这把短剑就和我现在手里的一样。（他触摸着手里的短剑。）现在这把短剑看起来血迹斑斑！仅夜黑得好像整个世界诡异得像死一般的寂静。狼在嚎叫着，我仿佛能感受到围绕在我身边的魔鬼，可我依旧在这里浪费着宝贵的时间。 |
| (A bell rings.) | | |
| | That's the signal from my wife. She has prepared everything. I'm going. I'll do it. That was the bell calling Duncan to heaven or to hell. | 这是我妻子的信号，她已经准备好了一切。我要去了，我一定能做到。那钟声响给Duncan，要唤他下地狱，或是送他上天堂。 |
| (Macbeth exits. Lady Macbeth enters.) | | |
| LADY MACBETH (Lady Macbeth thinks aloud.) | I've drugged the guards. They are fast asleep. Macbeth must be murdering Duncan | 我给守卫下过安眠药，他们已经睡着了。Macbeth一定是在这个时候谋杀Dun |

| | at this moment. | can。 |
|---|---|---|
| (Macbeth's voice is heard from backstage.) | | |
| MACBETH | Is anyone there? | 有人吗？ |
| (Macbeth enters with blood on his hands, carrying two daggers.) | | |
| LADY MACBETH | Macbeth! | Macbeth! |
| MACBETH (Looking at his hands) | This is a frightening sight. | 这是可怕的一幕。 |
| LADY MACBETH | Don't think about it so deeply, my dear. | 亲爱的，别想太多了。 |
| MACBETH | I thought I heard a voice say, "Macbeth won't sleep anymore. He's murdered sleep, and sleep is dead. Macbeth will never know sleep again." | 我想我听见一个声音在说"Macbeth再也不能入睡了，他谋杀了睡眠，而现在睡眠死了。Macbeth再也不会知道入睡了。" |
| LADY MACBETH | We cannot afford to talk or think like this – otherwise we'll go crazy. Why are you still holding the guards' daggers? Take them back. | 我们不能像这样讨论或者思考了 - 否则我们会疯的。你怎么还拿着守卫的短剑？快把它们放回去。 |
| MACBETH | I'm not going. | 我不会去。 |
| LADY MACBETH | Here, give them to me. | 来，把它们给我。 |
| (Lady Macbeth exits. Knocking is heard.) | | |
| MACBETH | What's that knocking noise? My hands might never come clean but will just keep turning the water red forever. | 那是什么敲击声？我的双手再也不干净了，但它们会一直把水染成赤红一片。 |

| | | |
|---|---|---|
| (Lady Macbeth enters.) | | |
| LADY MACBETH | Someone is knocking at the South Gate. Let's go back to our bedroom. A little water on our hands and we'll be fine. (Louder knocking is heard.) Quickly. We mustn't be caught here. Pull yourself together. | 有人在南门敲着门。让我们回卧室吧。只要一点水就能把我们的手洗干净了。（更大的敲门声响起。）快点儿，我们不能在这儿被抓住。振作起来。 |
| MACBETH | I wish they could wake up Duncan with their knocking. | 我希望他们能把Duncan敲醒。 |
| (They exit.) | | |
| ？ | | |

15

| ACT 2, Scene 2 | | |
|---|---|---|
| (The Porter enters the courtyard by the South Gate. Loud knocking is heard.) | | |
| PORTER | OK, OK! I'm coming! What's the rush? No time for jokes around here. A little comedy, that's what I need. All that knocking! I know. Knock, knock! Who's there? Lettuce. Lettuce who? Let us come in or we'll break the door down! Knock, knock! Who's there? Anita. Anita who? Anita come in. Last one. Knock, knock! Who's there? Theodore. Theodore who? Open the door! | 好啦，好啦！我来啦！有什么好急的呢？我们没时间在这儿开玩笑了，我只需要一点能逗乐的就行了。所有的敲门声我都听到，敲，再敲！谁在那儿？Lettuce。Lettuce是谁？让我们进来，否则我们会破门而入！敲，再敲！谁在那儿？Anita。Anita是谁？Anita最后个到了。敲，再敲！谁在那儿？Theodore。Theodore是谁？快开门！ |
| (The Porter opens the door. Macduff and Lennox enter.) | | |
| MACDUFF (To the Porter) | Is your master awake? | 你主人醒了吗？ |
| (Macbeth enters.) | | |
| We must have woken him up with our knocking. Here he comes. | | |
| (The Porter exits.) | | |
| LENNOX (To Macbeth) | Good morning, sir. | 早上好，先生。 |
| MACBETH | A good morning to you both. | 早上好，二位。 |

| | | |
|---|---|---|
| MACDUFF | Is the King awake yet? | 国王醒了吗？ |
| MACBETH | Not yet. | 还没有。 |
| MACDUFF | He asked me to wake him early. Let me go to him. | 他让我早点来叫他。我去找他吧。 |
| MACBETH | No, really. Don't trouble yourself. | 真的没有，别自找麻烦。 |
| MACDUFF | He asked me. I'll go. | 他叫我这么做的，我去了。 |
| (Exit Macduff.) | | |
| LENNOX | So, the King's traveling on today? | 国王今天启程吗？ |
| MACBETH | Right. That's what he said. | 对，他是这么说的。 |
| LENNOX | It's been a terrible night. The wind made a moaning sound all night, and we could hear an owl screeching. | 这是个可怕的夜晚。风呻吟了一晚上，我们可以听见猫头鹰的叫声。 |
| (Macduff enters.) | | |
| MACDUFF | It's horrible! I just can't believe it! | 太可怕了！我简直不敢相信！ |
| LENNOX and MACBETH | What's wrong? | 怎么了？ |
| MACDUFF | A dreadful murder! | 可怕的谋杀！ |
| LENNOX | Our King? | 我们的国王？ |
| MACDUFF | Yes! Go see it for yourselves. | 是的！你们自己去看看吧。 |
| (Macbeth and Lennox exit.) | | |
| | Wake up! Wake up, everyone! Murder! Murder! | 醒醒！大家都醒醒！有谋杀！有谋杀！ |
| (Lady Macbeth enters.) | | |
| LADY MACBETH | What's all the fuss? | 有什么大惊小怪的 |

| | | ？ |
|---|---|---|
| (Banquo enters.) | | |
| MACDUFF | Oh, Banquo, Banquo! Our King has been murdered! | 哦，Banquo，Banquo！我们的国王被谋杀了！ |
| LADY MACBETH | Oh, no! Not in our castle! | 哦，不！这不是在我们的城堡里！ |
| BANQUO | Macduff, tell me it's not true! | Macduff，告诉我这不是真的！ |
| (Macbeth, Lennox, and Rosse enter.) | | |
| MACBETH | If I had died an hour ago, I would have died a happy man. | 如果我在一个小时前死去，我便是幸福一生。 |
| (Malcolm and Donalbain enter.) | | |
| DONALBAIN | What's wrong? | 怎么了？ |
| MACDUFF | Your father has been murdered. | 你的父亲被谋杀了。 |
| MALCOLM | Who did it? | 谁干的？ |
| LENNOX | It looks like his guards did it, but we can't punish them now. Macbeth killed them. | 看上去像是他的守卫。但我们现在无法惩罚他们了，他们被Macbeth杀害了。 |
| MACBETH | I saw my innocent King lying there dead, and his murderers were still there. I was furious. | 我看到我那无辜的国王躺在那里，可杀死他的凶手却还站在那！我气坏了。 |
| LADY MACBETH | Oh! I feel quite faint! | 哦！我快要晕过去了！ |
| MACDUFF | Lady Macbeth needs help. | Macbeth夫人需要帮助。 |
| (Lady Macbeth exits, helped by Macbeth. Everyone exits except | | |

| | | |
|---|---|---|
| Malcolm and Donalbain.) | | |
| MALCOLM | What are we going to do? Whoever killed our father is going to try to kill us next. | 我们现在去做什么？无论是谁杀了我们的父亲接下来都是要对我们下手的。 |
| DONALBAIN | I don't trust anyone here anymore. We'll be safer if we're apart. You go to England. I'll go to Ireland. Let's not tell anybody we're going. | 我不再相信这里的任何人了，分开会使我们更安全。你去英格兰，而我去爱尔兰。别向任何人透露我们的去向。 |
| (The brothers exit in opposite directions.) ☐ | | |
| ACT 3, Scene 1 | | |
| (The palace at Forres owned by King Macbeth of Scotland. Banquo enters a reception hall.) | | |
| BANQUO (thinks aloud.) | Well, you've got it all now, Macbeth. You've been crowned King, just like those weird witches said. But I'm afraid you played dirty to get it. | 现在你得到一切了Macbeth。正如那些女巫所说你加冕为王，但我恐怕你因此用了些卑鄙肮脏的手段。 |
| (Macbeth enters wearing Duncan's crown, with Lennox, Rosse, and Lady Macbeth.) | | |
| MACBETH | And here's our special guest! Banquo, I want you to attend an | 这是我们特殊的客人！我今晚设有盛筵，Banquo，请你 |

| | | |
|---|---|---|
| | important dinner tonight. Are you going riding today? | 光临。今天下午你出去骑马么？ |
| BANQUO | Yes, I am, but if you want me at your feast, I'll be there. | 是的，但如果你希望我参加你的筵席，我会到场。 |
| MACBETH | Enjoy your ride. Is your son Fleance going? | 享受你的骑行吧。你儿子Fleance去么？ |
| BANQUO | Yes. | 去的。 |
| (Banquo bows and exits.) | | |
| MACBETH | Now then, everyone. Your time is your own until we dine at 7 o'clock sharp. | 那么各位，在晚上7点整开餐之前享受属于你们自己的时间吧。 |
| (Everyone exits except Macbeth.) | | |
| MACBETH (thinks aloud) | So far so good. But Banquo could destroy me. The witches said his sons would be kings after me. If that's true, I've risked my life for his sons. Killed innocent Duncan for Banquo's sons. Given up my honor, just for them. To make them kings. | 到目前为止一切都很好，但是Banquo可能毁了我。那些女巫说他的儿子会成为下一任国王。如果这是真的话，那我就是在用自己的生命去为他的儿子冒险。放弃了我的荣誉而杀害了无辜的Duncan，只是为了让Banquo的儿子成为国王。 |
| (A knock is heard.) | | |
| Who's there? | | |
| (Two murderers enter.) | | |
| MURDERER 1 | You asked us to come. | 是你叫我们来的。 |

20

| MACBETH | Have you thought over what I said yesterday about Banquo being the bad guy and not me? | 你们可曾考虑过我昨天说的那些关于Banquo才是真正的恶人而不是我吗？ |
|---|---|---|
| MURDERER 2 | We've got nothing to lose, so who cares? | 我们没什么好失去的，谁又在意那些呢？ |
| MACBETH | But you do know that Banquo is your enemy, don't you? | 但是你们知道Banquo是你们的敌人，不是吗？ |
| MURDERER 1 | Yeah, yeah. | 对啊。 |
| MACBETH | You must be sure to kill Banquo and his son, Fleance. I don't want any foul-ups. Now get out of sight. Do a good job. | 你们必须确保杀了Banquo和他的儿子Fleance，并且我不希望出现任何疏忽差错。现在走出我的视线吧，好好干。 |
| (All exit.) | | |
| ⍰ | | |

| ACT 3, Scene 2 | | |
|---|---|---|
| (The palace at Forres. Eight chairs are brought onstage for the banquet. Macbeth, Lady Macbeth, and several lords<br><br>Rosse, Lennox, Angus, and Menteith enter the banquet hall.) | | |
| MACBETH | Welcome, everyone. You know your places. Sit yourselves down. | 欢迎各位光临。你们知道自己该坐哪儿，找座位坐下。 |
| (Lady Macbeth, Rosse, Lennox, Angus, and Menteith seat themselves.) | | |
| | I would like this to be a happy occasion, a celebration of the new order in Scotland. | 我希望这是个愉快的场合，来庆祝苏格兰新体制的诞生。 |
| (Murderer 1 appears at the doorway.) | | |
| | Enjoy yourselves! | 玩儿的开心些！ |
| (Macbeth goes to the doorway.) | | |
| | You've got blood on your face. | 你的脸上有血。 |
| MURDERER 1 | It must be Banquo's. Banquo is dead. I cut his throat. But Fleance escaped, my Lord. | 这应该是Banquo的血，Banquo已经死了。启禀陛下，我砍断了他的喉咙，可Fleance逃了。 |
| MACBETH | Oh, no! With him alive, I am still in danger. Still, he's too | 哦，不！只要他还活着我就依旧有危险，但现在他还太 |

| | | |
|---|---|---|
| | young to be dangerous yet. Come and see me tomorrow. | 年轻不足以造成威胁。明天再来见我吧。 |
| (Murderer 1 exits.) | | |
| LADY MACBETH (Coming over to Macbeth) | Don't leave your guests alone like this. You didn't invite them just to eat – we're supposed to be celebrating. | 不要这样让你的客人独处。你还没请他们开始用餐 - 我们应该开始庆祝了。 |
| MACBETH (To the lords) | Why isn't Banquo here? It's rude and unkind of him to miss this important occasion. | Banquo怎么不在这儿？这种粗鲁和无理的行为会使他错过这重要的场合。 |
| ROSSE | Come, join us, sir. | 到我们当中来吧，先生。 |
| (The ghost of Banquo enters and sits in Macbeth's place.) | | |
| MACBETH (Seeing the ghost) | Which one of you did this? | 这是谁干的？ |
| ROSSE | What do you mean, my Lord? | 我的陛下，您这是什么意思？ |
| LENNOX | Gentlemen, the King is unwell. | 先生们，国王有些身体不适。 |
| (Lennox stands, ready to leave. Lady Macbeth goes to Macbeth.) | | |
| LADY MACBETH | No, no! He is sometimes like this. He's always had these strange turns, ever since he was a boy. It will pass. Don't pay any attention. (Aside to Macbeth) What are | 不，不！他有时候就是这样，当他是个小男孩时就总是有这些奇怪的转变。等一会就好了，大家别在意。（对旁边的Macbeth）你在干什 |

| | you doing now? | 么？ |
|---|---|---|
| MACBETH | I'm looking at a dead man. Look! Right there! We should cut dead people into little pieces so that the parts can never make a whole ghost. | 我看到个死人，看，就在那儿！我们应该将尸体切成小块，让这些小块再也无法形成完整的鬼魂。 |
| (The ghost of Banquo leaves.) | | |
| LADY MACBETH | Your guests are missing you, dear husband. | 亲爱的丈夫，您的客人还等着你呢。 |
| MACBETH (To the guests) | I'm sorry. I do have this strange illness. People who know me well don't worry about it. Let me sit down. (The Macbeths and Lennox sit down.) Love and health to one and all. Bring me some wine! | 我很抱歉。我确实有这种奇怪的病，但凡是了解我的人都不会在意。让我坐会。（Macbeth夫妇和Lennox坐下。）祝每一位朋友幸福健康！给我拿些酒来！ |
| (A wine server enters and exits as the ghost reenters.) | | |
| | I propose a toast to you, my dear friends. To our missing friend, Banquo—I wish he were here now—and to you all! | 我向大家提议，为我亲爱的朋友们，还有失踪的Banquo举杯 - 但愿他在座 - 敬祝大家！ |
| LORDS | To Macbeth! | 敬祝Macbeth！ |

| | | |
|---|---|---|
| (Macbeth sees the ghost.) | | |
| MACBETH<br><br>(The lords stand, ready to leave.) | Go! Get out of my sight! Crawl into your grave! Your blood is cold! Your eyes are blind! Don't stare at me! | 滚开！从我的视线中消失！爬到你的坟墓里去！你的血是冷的！你的眼睛是瞎的！不要盯着我！ |
| LADY MACBETH | Just think of him as slightly eccentric. | 就当他有点怪就好了。 |
| MACBETH | If you were alive, I'd kill you. Go, go! Get out of here! | 如果你还活着，我会杀了你的。滚！快离开这！ |
| (The ghost exits.) | | |
| | Ah, that's better. More normal. Please, stay! (The lords sit down again, but they are very puzzled by Macbeth's behavior.) | 啊，现在好点了，正常多了。请坐！（贵族们再次坐下，但大家对Macbeth的行为十分不解。） |
| LADY MACBETH<br>(To Macbeth) | You've turned this night into quite a circus. | 你将今晚变成了一场马戏表演。 |
| MACBETH | How can you look so calm when these sights make me sick with terror? | 这些看上去令我感到恐怖的东西，你见了怎么会面不改色？ |
| LADY MACBETH | He's having a bad attack. Good night. Please don't be formal. Just go. Good night to you all. | 他发作的更糟了。晚安各位，不必拘泥，退席就行了，大家晚安。 |
| (All exit except the Macbeths.) | | |
| MACBETH | Why didn't Macduff come tonight? I don't trust anyone. Early | 今晚Macduff怎么没来？我不再相信任何人了，明天一早 |

| | | |
|---|---|---|
| | tomorrow morning I'm going to find those weird witches. I want to know the worst. | 我要去寻找那些怪异的女巫，我想知道最坏的结果。 |
| LADY MACBETH | You need sleep. | 你需要睡了。 |
| MACBETH | I'm a beginner; that's my problem. It's all so new to me. Once I get used to this kind of life, I'll be fine. It's all so new to us. | 我的问题就在这，我是个初学者，这一切对我来说都如此的新鲜。一旦我习惯了这样的生活，我就会好起来的。这一切对我们来说都是如此的新鲜。 |
| (The Macbeths exit. The eight chairs are taken offstage.) | | |
| 🔲 | | |
| ACT 4 | | |
| (Thunder is heard. Three witches enter a wild part of the Scottish woods and dance in a circle around a boiling cauldron.) | | |
| ALL THREE WITCHES | Hands around the cauldron go! In the poisoned entrails throw! Hubble, double, toil and trouble! Fire blaze! Macbeth is crazed! | 双手围着煮锅走！毒肝毒脏向锅里投！加倍加倍努力干！燃烧吧！Macbeth已经疯狂了！ |
| WITCH 1 | Scale of dragon, tooth of wolf, Blood of dog, horse's hoof, Finger of a strangled baby, Monkey's paw? No . . . | 巨龙鳞，豺狼牙，恶狗血，弩马蹄，被勒死婴儿的手指，猴子得手爪？哦不，..可能也需要。 |

| | well, maybe. | |
|---|---|---|
| ALL THREE WITCHES | Hubble, double toil and trouble! Fire blaze! Macbeth is crazed! | 加倍加倍努力干！燃烧吧！Macbeth已经疯狂了！ |
| WITCH 2 | Cool it with a kitten's blood. Now the spell is sure and good. | 用点小猫血才能凝固，现在巫术已经稳定了。 |
| WITCH 3 | By the tingling in my fingers, I know that someone evil lingers. | 我的手指刺痛不散，我感觉到有些恶灵在这逗留。 |
| (Macbeth enters.) | | |
| MACBETH | There you are! What are you doing? | 找到你了！你在干什么？ |
| ALL THREE WITCHES | An act without a name. | 一件无名的事。 |
| MACBETH | I don't care what you are doing. But answer my questions. | 我不在乎你们在做什么，只要回答我的问题就行。 |
| WITCH 3 | Spirits will appear, and they'll answer your questions through us. Watch! . . . See? The head of an armed soldier, wearing a helmet. | 灵魂会出现，代替我们回答你的问题。看到了吗？那个带着头盔的首级。 |
| WITCH 1 | You don't have to ask anything. They read your mind. He says, "Macbeth! Macbeth! Watch out for Macduff!" | 他知道你的心事，你什么都不用问。听他说："Macbeth! Macbeth!留心Macduff!" |

| WITCH 2 | Here's a more powerful spirit, a child covered with blood. In a tiny, childlike voice, he says, "Macbeth! You can live dangerously because no one born by a woman can harm you." | 现在是更强大的灵魂，那个浴血婴孩。用微弱的稚气的声音说着："Macbeth!你可以活在危险之中，因为没有女人生出来的人能伤害你。" |
|---|---|---|
| MACBETH | What's this! A child crowned like a king, carrying a tree? | 这是什么！这头戴王冕又手执树枝的幼童是谁？ |
| WITCH 3 | Don't talk! Listen! This spirit says, "Be confident, Macbeth. Be aggressive. No harm will come to you until Birnam Wood picks up and moves to Dunsinane Hill." | 别说话尽管听！灵魂说着："自信些强势些Macbeth。没有什么能伤害你，除非等到Birnam大森林移到Dunsinane高山上。" |
| MACBETH | Well, that's not going to happen. Whoever heard of all the trees in a wood deciding to relocate? Good, this is just what I wanted to hear. But tell me one more thing. Will Banquo's son ever be King of Scotland? | 永远不会有的事，谁听说过森林会移动？不错，这就是我想听到的。但请再告诉我，Banquo的子孙终将成为苏格兰的国王吗？ |
| ALL THREE WITCHES | No more! Use your eyes. Break your heart. Listen once more, then depart! | 别再多问了！用眼睛看，用心感受，再听一遍，然后就离开吧！ |
| (Macbeth sees apparitions in the sky.) | | |
| MACBETH | Eight kings walking in a procession. And they | 八代国王在游行着，他们都像Banquo |

| | | |
|---|---|---|
| | all look like Banquo! They are his children! What a ghastly sight! You filthy hags! | ！他们是他的后代！多么可怕的景象！你这龌龊的妖婆！ |
| (The witches disappear. Lennox enters.) | | |
| Did you see them? | | |
| LENNOX | Who? No. My Lord, I've come to tell you that Macduff escaped to England. | 谁？没看见，陛下。我是来告诉您Macduff逃到英格兰去了。 |

| | | |
|---|---|---|
| MACBETH (thinks aloud.) | From now on, there's no stopping me. I shall do the very first thing that comes into my head. And I'll start by having Macduff's castle torn apart. I want his wife and children dead. | 从现在起任何事都不能阻止我，我要做现在在我脑海盘旋的第一件事。我要从让Macduff的城堡四分五裂开始，我要让他的妻子和孩子死亡。 |
| (Macbeth exits.) | | |
| ⬚ | | |
| ACT 5, Scene 1 | | |
| (Macbeth's castle in Dunsinane. The doctor and the Lady-in-Waiting enter a hallway outside Lady Macbeth's bedroom.) | | |
| DOCTOR | When did Lady Macbeth last walk in her sleep? | Macbeth夫人上一次梦游是什么时候？ |
| LADY-IN-WAITING | She does it every night, sir. | 她每晚都会梦游，先生。 |
| DOCTOR | That is not normal . . . When she sleepwalks, does she speak? | 这真奇怪.... . 当她梦游时她说话吗？ |
| LADY-IN-WAITING | Yes, but I don't think I should repeat what she says. | 说的，但我不认为我应该重复她说的话。 |
| (Lady Macbeth enters, carrying a candle. She paces backward and forward and then places the candle on the floor while she rubs her hands, as if washing them.) | | |
| DOCTOR | How did she get that | 她怎么拿到蜡烛的 |

| | candle? | ？ |
|---|---|---|
| LADY-IN-WAITING | She's always had one by her side, sir. She can't bear the darkness. | 就在她身边，先生。她不能忍受黑暗。 |
| DOCTOR | What's she doing now? Why is she rubbing her hands together? | 她在做什么呢？为什么一直在搓手？ |
| LADY-IN-WAITING | She's always doing that. Sometimes she does it for fifteen minutes at a time. | 这是她惯常动作。有时她能这样维持一刻钟之久。 |

| LADY MACBETH | Still a spot here. Come out, stain. One, two, we should be doing it now. Hell's a dark place. Shame, husband! You are a soldier, but afraid. Doesn't matter who suspects us. Who could have dreamed the old king had so much blood in him? | 这还有个斑点。出来吧色斑。一，二，到下手的时候了。地狱是黑暗的！呸，丈夫！一个军人，还害怕？别担心谁会怀疑到我们身上，谁能想到那个老头子有那么多的血啊？ |
|---|---|---|
| DOCTOR | Did you hear that! | 你听见这话了么！ |
| LADY MACBETH | The Thane of Fife, he had a wife. Where is she now? Won't I ever get these hands clean? Sleep, my lord, sleep. Why can't you sleep? I can still smell blood. Oh! Wash your hands! Get ready for bed! Don't look so pale. Banquo's dead. He can't touch you now. | Fife的伯爵曾有位夫人，如今在哪里？这双手永远洗不干净了吗？睡吧，我的王，快睡吧，你为何迟迟不能入睡？我依旧能闻到血腥味，哦！快去把手洗洗然后准备上床睡觉！别看上去这么苍白，Banquo已经死了，他碰不到你了。 |
| (Lady Macbeth picks up the candle and exits.) | | |
| DOCTOR | She doesn't need me. She needs God. Look after her. Any object that could harm her should be removed. Good night. | 她不需要我，她需要上帝。好好照顾她吧，挪去一切她可以伤害自己的东西。晚安。 |
| LADY-IN-WAITING | Thank you. Good night, Doctor. | 谢谢你，先生，晚安。 |
| (Lady-in-Waiting and | | |

| | | |
|---|---|---|
| Doctor exit in opposite directions.) | | |
| ACT 5, Scene 2 | | |
| (Dunsinane. Macbeth and the Doctor enter another room in the castle.) | | |
| MACBETH | Don't tell me any more news. I have nothing to fear until Birnam Wood moves to Dunsinane Hill. The powerful spirits who know everything said to me, "Macbeth! You can live dangerously because no one who was "born by a woman" can harm you." So you see I've got nothing to fear. | 不必再来报告，除非等到Birnam大森林移到Dunsinane高山上，我就没什么好怕的。那预知的强大灵魂曾向我说过："Macbeth!你可以活在危险之中，因为没有女人生出来的人能伤害你。"看吧，我没什么好怕的。 |

| | | |
|---|---|---|
| (A Messenger enters. For a moment, he can't speak.) | | |
| MACBETH | What's the matter? Why do you look as white as a goose? | 怎么了？你脸色怎么看上去像只白鹅？ |
| MESSENGER | My Lord Macbeth! There are ten thousand . . . | 我亲爱的陛下，有一万个….. |
| MACBETH | Ten thousand geese? | 一万只鹅？ |
| MESSENGER | No, ten thousand soldiers. | 不，一万个士兵啊。 |
| MACBETH | Whose soldiers, you fool? | 你这个蠢蛋，是谁的士兵？ |
| MESSENGER | Malcolm, Macduff, Lennox, and the English army, my Lord, They're marching this way! | Malcolm、Macduff、Lennox、还有英国军队。我的陛下，他们正向我们进军！ |
| MACBETH | I'll fight them. | 我会打败他们。 |
| (Messenger exits.) | | |
| How is your patient, Doctor? | | |
| DOCTOR | Not really sick, my Lord, but very disturbed by violent thoughts. | 陛下，她的病不要紧的，但她的精神错乱以致幻象丛生。 |
| MACBETH | Cure her. | 那就治好她。 |
| DOCTOR | The patient needs God. | 病人需要的是上帝。 |
| MACBETH | Medicine isn't much help, then. Still, if you could cure my country of its ills, make Scotland healthy again, I'd applaud non-stop. | 药物已经不起作用了。但如果你仍能医治好我的国家，使苏格兰再次恢复繁盛，我会再度给你不息的掌声。 |
| (They exit.) | | |

| ? | | |
|---|---|---|
| ACT 5, Scene 3 | | |
| (The countryside near Birnam Wood. Malcolm, Macduff, and Rosse are marching toward Macbeth's castle.) | | |
| MACDUFF | What's this wood we're coming up to? | 前面快到的是什么森林？ |
| ROSSE | It's Birnam Wood. | 是 Birnam 森林。 |

| MALCOLM | I've got an idea. I want every soldier to cut down a big branch and carry it in front of himself so that our enemy, Macbeth, won't know how many of us are coming. | 我有个主意。我希望每个士兵砍下一个大树支，在面前擎着，这样便可以遮掩我们的人数，而我们的敌人Macbeth，就不会知道我们到底来了多少人。 |
|---|---|---|
| (They exit.) | | |
| ⏷ | | |
| ACT 5, Scene 4 | | |
| (Macbeth's castle. Macbeth and Seyton enter.) | | |
| MACBETH | We have everything we need inside this castle. Bring up the drawbridge. Let them lay siege to our castle. | 城堡里有我们需要的一切东西，把吊桥拿来，让他们围困我们的城堡吧。 |
| (A woman's scream is heard.) | | |
| | What was that? Investigate that noise, Seyton. | 那是什么声音？去查查，Seyton。 |
| (Seyton exits.) | | |
| | It used to make my flesh creep to hear a scream like that. But now, such horrors are quite common. | 这样的尖叫曾让我感到毛骨悚然，但现在已经不会再使我惊惶了。 |
| (Seyton reenters.) | | |
| SEYTON | The Queen is dead, my Lord. | 陛下，王后死了。 |
| MACBETH | I wish she had died when there was time to grieve properly. Life just goes on and on. The days come and | 我希望她可以在我有时间去悲伤的时候死去。生活还是要继续，一天天来了又走，走了又来 |

|  | go, come and go. Life's is being an actor in a play. Your worry about it, you do it, you have your moment, and then it's over. The end. All the noise and anger . . . it doesn't mean a thing. | 。生活就像一位演员，你为它担心，为它做些什么，你有属于你的时间，最后一切都结束了。剧终的时候，所有的嘈杂和愤怒..都没有任何意义。 |
|---|---|---|
| (A Messenger enters.) |  |  |
| What is it? |  |  |

| MESSENGER | This is going to sound very strange, Sir, but as I was keeping watch just now, I saw Birnam Wood moving toward the castle. | 陛下，这一切听上去非常奇怪，但当我刚才在守望的时候，我看到Birnam森林在向我们的城堡移动。 |
|---|---|---|
| MACBETH | If you're lying, I'll hang you from a tree. If you're not, I don't care if you hang me. I'm beginning to doubt those witches. "Be confident, Macbeth. Be aggressive. No harm will come to you until Birnam Wood picks up and moves to Dunsinane Hill." And now the Wood is approaching Dunsinane Hill. There's nothing to do but pick up our weapons and fight! Help me on with my armor! | 如果你在撒谎，我就把你吊在一棵树上，我并不在乎你也这么对我。我开始怀疑那些巫婆说的话了："自信些强势些Macbeth。没有什么能伤害你，除非等到Birnam大森林移到Dunsinane高山上。"如今树林真的来到了Dunsinane高山上，除了拿起兵器战斗我们无事可做！帮我披上我的盔甲！ |
| (They exit.) | | |
| ⏍ | | |
| ACT 5, Scene 5 | | |
| (Menteith and Seyton enter and fight each other. Then Macbeth and Siward enter and fight each other.) | | |
| SIWARD | You murderer! | 你这个凶手！ |
| (Macbeth and Siward fight. Menteith and Seyton exit, fighting. Macbeth kills Siward.) | | |

| MACBETH | You were born by a woman. | 你可是女人生的。 |
|---|---|---|
| (Macduff enters.) | | |
| | Of everyone, I didn't want to meet you, Macduff. I'm already covered in your family's blood. | 所有人中我最不想见的就是你，Macduff。我的双手已经沾满了你家族的鲜血。 |
| MACDUFF | What makes you think you'll win this fight? | 是什么让你觉得你能赢得这场战斗？ |
| MACBETH | You can't kill me. I have a charmed life. The witches said that only a man not born by a woman could kill me. | 你杀不了我，因为我有着魔咒般的生命。女巫说只有不是女人所生的人可以杀了我。 |
| MACDUFF | Your charmed life is over, Macbeth. Listen to this | 听听这声音吧Macbeth，你那魔咒般的生命该结束了。 |
| | My mother didn't give birth to me naturally. I was removed from her by a doctor! | 我的母亲并没有顺产下我，我是医生从母亲子宫里剖出来的。 |
| MACBETH | You can't trick me by playing with words, Macduff. I shall fight you to the death – your death! | 你这些话是骗不了我的Macduff。我会战斗到死亡的 - 到你的死亡！ |
| (They exit, fighting.) | | |
| ⬚ | | |
| ACT 5, Scene 6 | | |
| (Malcolm, Menteith, and Lords 4, 5, 6, 7, and 8 enter and are met by Macduff, who is splattered with | | |

39

| | | |
|---|---|---|
| blood.) | | |
| MACDUFF | Welcome, my King, because that's what you are now. Macbeth is dead. We are free! Malcolm, you are the King of Scotland! | 欢迎您，我的陛下！因为你是国王了！Macbeth死了，我们自由了！Malcolm，你是苏格兰的国王！ |
| ALL | Long live the King! | 国王万岁！ |
| MALCOLM | My only regret is that some of our dear friends had to die. Everyone who hid from Macbeth and lived in fear of him must be told that the butcher and his evil queen are dead. I thank you, one and all, and invite you to Scone, where I will be crowned King of Scotland. | 我唯一的遗憾是那些我们挚友的离去。每一位被Macbeth藏起来的和在他的恐惧下生活的人都应该知道这位残忍的刽子手和他邪恶的王后已经死了。我真心的感谢并邀请你们在场的每一位人来Scone，那个我会被加冕为苏格兰王的地方！ |
| (They all exit. END OF PLAY.) | | |

## ACT ONE, Scene One

| | |
|---|---|
| **Witches** | **Physical Action**: To perform a magic ritual |
| | **Emotional Action**: To meddle in the lives of those less powerful |
| | **It Reminds Me Of**: Teasing some younger kids with the "sitting in a tree, k-i-s-s-i-n-g" rhyme |

(The place is a field in Scotland. Three witches enter, running. They join hands and circle very fast while counting to ten silently. At ten, they stop. They are weird!)

**WITCH 1:** You, you, and me; we three, let's see . . .

**WITCH 2:** We'll do this again.

**WITCH 3:** But when? In thunder, lightning, or rain?

**WITCH 1:** When the hurlyburly's over.

**WITCH 2:** When they've got what they want and lost it.

**WITCH 3:** Tonight.

**WITCH 1:** In the woods.

**WITCH 2:** And there we'll meet Macbeth {mehk-BETH}.

**ALL THREE WITCHES:** Good looks bad, and bad looks good.

**WITCH 3:** Let's move and go.

**WITCH 1:** And wait.

**WITCH 2:** And watch.

(They exit suddenly, running.)

## ACT ONE, Scene Two

| | |
|---|---|
| **Soldier** | **Physical Action**: To report the news to the King |
| | **Emotional Action**: To make sure the most powerful person in my life gets an honest report of what's happening |
| | **It Reminds Me Of**: Telling my father exactly how I'm doing in math so he knows that I really am paying attention to it |
| **King Duncan** | **Physical Action**: To get more news about the battle |
| | **Emotional Action**: To make sure people who support me are cared for |
| | **It Reminds Me Of**: Being captain of the soccer team and making sure an injured player was OK before the game continued |
| **Rosse, Lennox** | **Physical Action**: To follow King Duncan |
| | **Emotional Action**: To be ready to obey the King's orders |
| | **It Reminds Me Of**: Waiting for the teacher to get his papers organized when we were about to have a test |

(A badly wounded soldier enters first. Then King Duncan of Scotland enters, followed by Rosse and Lennox. They are close to the battlefield.)

**KING DUNCAN:** I can see that you are hurt badly by the fighting, soldier, but can you report how we are doing against the rebellious Macdonwald {mehk-DON-wald}? Speak!

**SOLDIER:** Your generals are doing a great job out there, King Duncan. Macbeth has killed that upstart Macdonwald. Macbeth stuck Macdonwald's head on the end of a pole to encourage his own men.

**KING DUNCAN:** Macbeth is a brave man.

**SOLDIER:** Your thane of Cawdor {KAH-door} is another story. He has helped the enemy. But Macbeth and Banquo {BAN-kwoe} have already made the traitor suffer.

**KING DUNCAN:** The Thane of Cawdor is a traitor, and I will see that he dies because of it. Macbeth will be the new Thane of Cawdor. Macbeth deserves the honor.

# ACT ONE, Scene Three

| | |
|---|---|
| **Witches** | **Physical Action**: To confront Macbeth and Banquo with predictions |
| | **Emotional Action**: To meddle in the lives of those less powerful |
| | **It Reminds Me Of**: Teasing my friends by telling them part of a secret but not the whole secret |
| **Macbeth** | **Physical Action**: To stay strong while seeing witches |
| | **Emotional Action**: To understand whether this is a real opportunity |
| | **It Reminds Me Of**: Winning a talent contest and wondering whether I could really be in show business |
| **Banquo** | **Physical Action**: To cope with seeing witches |
| | **Emotional Action**: To urge Macbeth not to do anything foolish based on what the witches say |
| | **It Reminds Me Of**: Telling a friend not to drive so fast just because he was borrowing his father's powerful car |
| **Rosse** | **Physical Action**: To deliver a message to Macbeth |
| | **Emotional Action**: To do my duty quickly |
| | **It Reminds Me Of**: Being told to |

| | clean my room and it was only a five-minute job |
| --- | --- |

(The three witches enter a wild part of the woods.)

**WITCH 1:** Where have you been?

**WITCH 2:** Meddling.

**WITCH 3:** And you?

**WITCH 1:** About. Sailing in a boat full of holes. Running like a rat without a tail.

**WITCH 2:** Look at this!

**WITCH 3:** A man's thumb!

**ALL THREE WITCHES:** Mmmmmm!

**WITCH 1:** Shh! Here comes Macbeth!

(Macbeth and Banquo enter.)

**MACBETH:** We've had a good day. But this fog is bad.

(Banquo sees the witches.)

**BANQUO:** What the . . . Are you dead or alive?

**WITCH 1:** Welcome, Macbeth, than of Glamis {GLAH-mis}!

**WITCH 2:** Welcome, Macbeth, thane of Cawdor!

**WITCH 3:** Welcome, Macbeth, soon to be called king!

**MACBETH:** No!

**BANQUO:** What's wrong? "King." Sounds good to me.

**WITCH 1:** Welcome!

**WITCH 2:** Welcome!

**WITCH 3:** Welcome!

**WITCH 1:** (To Banquo) Less than Macbeth, but more.

**WITCH 2:** Not as happy, but so much happier.

**WITCH 3:** Not king, but father of kings.

(The witches disappear.)

**MACBETH:** Come back here! What do you mean? The Thane of Cawdor and King Duncan are still alive!

**BANQUO:** There are some weird things in this world, and we just saw three of them.

**MACBETH:** They just said your children would be kings.

**BANQUO:** And you'd be Thane of Cawdor and then king. Who's there?

(Rosse enters.)

**ROSSE:** I am Rosse {ROHS}, a Scottish nobleman. I've been sent from the King to tell you that the traitor once known as the Thane of Cawdor is dead. You, Macbeth, have been named the new Thane of Cawdor.

(Rosse exits.)

**MACBETH:** Maybe your children will be kings.

**BANQUO:** It was a coincidence, Macbeth. Forget those evil creatures, or you'll regret it. I'll see you in King Duncan's palace.

(Banquo exits.)

**MACBETH:** Are these supernatural creatures evil or good? They told me good news, but they scare me. Maybe I will be made king, just as I was made Thane of Cawdor. I must talk to Lady Macbeth.

(Macbeth exits.)

| | |
|---|---|
| **Lady Macbeth** | **Physical Action**: To prepare for Macbeth's return from the war |
| | **Emotional Action**: To make sure the person I love does everything he should to succeed in life |
| | **It Reminds Me Of**: Making sure my boyfriend went to his math tutor every day instead of letting him go to the mall with me |
| **Macbeth** | **Physical Action**: To bring Lady Macbeth up-to-date |
| | **Emotional Action**: To find out whether a person I care for really wants me to do something I know is wrong |
| | **It Reminds Me Of**: Being asked to cut classes by my best friend |

(Macbeth's castle in Inverness, Scotland. Lady Macbeth enters, reading a letter from Macbeth.)

**LADY MACBETH:** I saw the witches the day I was made Thane of Cawdor. They predicted my new title. They also said I'd be called king. I knew this would make you happy, and I couldn't wait to tell you. I am on my way to you now, and King Duncan is following close behind me. Prepare the castle for our important visitor. (Now, Lady Macbeth thinks aloud to herself.) We must make our move now, Macbeth, but you worry me. You want to be great, and you're ambitious, but you just aren't quite evil enough to do what it takes to become king. I shall have to forget that I'm a woman for a while. I must be strong enough for two; otherwise, Macbeth will never be king. I must be cruel.

(Macbeth enters.)

Welcome, my dear and honored husband. Things are working out well for us.

**MACBETH:** Yes, but there is bad news. Malcolm has been made Prince of Cumberland. That means Malcolm will be the next King of Scotland – unless I stop him.

**LADY MACBETH:** When is King Duncan leaving our castle?

**MACBETH:** Tomorrow.

**LADY MACBETH:** That's what he thinks. Prepare for our regal visitor. Look happy.

**MACBETH:** We'll have to talk about this some more.

**LADY MACBETH:** I'll take care of this. But, for goodness' sake, look happy.

(They exit.)

## ACT ONE, Scene Five

| | |
|---|---|
| **King Duncan, Banquo** | **Physical Action**: To arrive at Macbeth's castle |
| | **Emotional Action**: To get ready to relax with people I like and trust |
| | **It Reminds Me Of**: Going to my best friend's house to watch a great movie |
| **Rosse, Lennox** | **Physical Action**: To follow King Duncan |
| | **Emotional Action**: To be ready to obey the King's orders |
| | **It Reminds Me Of**: Playing touch football and getting ready to hear the quarterback call the play |
| **Lady Macbeth** | **Physical Action**: To greet King Duncan |
| | **Emotional Action**: To make sure King Duncan feels welcome |
| | **It Reminds Me Of**: Pretending to be happy to see the dentist |

(Inverness, King Duncan, Rosse, Banquo, and Lennox enter the grounds of Macbeth's castle.)

**KING DUNCAN:** This castle was built in a beautiful place.

**BANQUO:** It's so peaceful here.

(Lady Macbeth enters.)

**KING DUNCAN:** Our good hostess! Give me your hand, good lady, and lead us to our noble host, the Thane of Cawdor.

(They exit.)

## ACT ONE, Scene Six

| | |
|---|---|
| **Macbeth** | **Physical Action**: To get away by myself |
| | **Emotional Action**: To calm down and try to think clearly |
| | **It Reminds Me Of**: Trying to figure out whether what I wanted to do was right or wrong and needing some time alone to think about it |
| **Lady Macbeth** | **Physical Action**: To follow Macbeth and help him think |
| | **Emotional Action**: To make sure a person very important to me doesn't back out of a commitment |
| | **It Reminds Me Of**: Being worried that my older sister was going to back out of taking me to the beach with her |

(Inverness. Macbeth enters a room leading off the dining room.)

**MACBETH:** (Macbeth thinks aloud to himself.) If I'm going to do it, I'd better get it over with quickly. But I am his cousin, I am his honored subject, and I am his host. Duncan trusts me. He's such a gentle and an honest king. The only thing that makes me want to kill Duncan is my ambition.

(Lady Macbeth enters.)

**LADY MACBETH:** What are you doing out here?

**MACBETH:** I can't see this thing through. He's been too

good to me.

**LADY MACBETH:** Do you want to live the rest of your life saying, "I might have been king. I could have been king if I'd dared to be"?

**MACBETH:** Shut up, woman! I can only do what a man can do. If I did more, I'd be a monster.

**LADY MACBETH:** No. When you were planning the murder, then you were a man. Now that Duncan is here, you're a bowl of Jell-O!

**MACBETH:** But what if something goes wrong?

**LADY MACBETH:** It won't. I'll put something in the guards' drinks that will make them sleep. Then you can stab Duncan with the guards' own daggers, and in the morning, it'll look like the guards did it.

**MACBETH:** OK. I'll do it. Let's get back to him now. The fake expressions on our faces must hide the real feelings and plans we have.

(They exit.)

## ACT TWO, Scene One

| | |
|---|---|
| **Macbeth** | **Physical Action**: To murder the King |
| | **Emotional Action**: To do what I have promised to do despite my misgivings |
| | **It Reminds Me Of**: Telling my mom I have no homework and then feeling I should be doing my homework |
| **Lady Macbeth** | **Physical Action**: To help Macbeth murder the King |
| | **Emotional Action**: To make sure the most important person in my life doesn't back out of doing something important for himself |
| | **It Reminds Me Of**: Taking my little sister to the tryouts for the school play and encouraging her to go onstage when she feels shy |

(Inverness. Macbeth enters the hallway outside King Duncan's bedroom.)

**MACBETH:** (Macbeth thinks aloud to himself.) Am I imagining things? I could swear there is a dagger right there in front of me, pointing the way to Duncan's bedroom. A dagger just as real as this one. (He feels his own dagger.) And now it looks bloodstained! It's so dark tonight that the whole world seems strangely dead. The wolves are howling. It's as if I could feel evil all around me. But I'm wasting precious time here.

(A bell rings.)

That's the signal from my wife. She has prepared everything. I'm going. I'll do it. That was the bell calling Duncan to heaven or to hell.

(Macbeth exits. Lady Macbeth enters.)

**LADY MACBETH:** (Lady Macbeth thinks aloud.) I've drugged the guards. They are fast asleep. Macbeth must be murdering Duncan at this moment.

(Macbeth's voice is heard from backstage.)

**MACBETH:** Is anyone there?

(Macbeth enters with blood [catsup] on his hands, carrying two daggers.)

**LADY MACBETH:** Macbeth!

**MACBETH:** (Looking at his hands) This is a frightening sight.

**LADY MACBETH:** Don't think about it so deeply, my dear.

**MACBETH:** I thought I heard a voice say, "Macbeth won't sleep anymore. He's murdered sleep, and sleep is dead. Macbeth will never know sleep again.

**LADY MACBETH:** We cannot afford to talk or think like this – otherwise we'll go crazy. Why are you still holding the guards' daggers? Take them back.

**MACBETH:** I'm not going.

**LADY MACBETH:** Here, give them to me.

(Lady Macbeth exits. Knocking is heard.)

**MACBETH:** What's that knocking noise? (Still staring at his hands) My hands might never come clean but will just keep turning the water red forever.

(Lady Macbeth enters.)

**LADY MACBETH:** Someone is knocking at the South Gate. Let's go back to our bedroom. A little water on our hands and we'll be fine. (Louder knocking is heard.) Quickly. We mustn't be caught here. Pull yourself together.

**MACBETH:** I wish they could wake up Duncan with their knocking.

(They exit.)

## ACT TWO, Scene Two

| | |
|---|---|
| **Porter** | **Physical Action**: To answer the door |
| | **Emotional Action**: To keep a sense of humor about this unpleasant job |
| | **It Reminds Me Of**: Having to clean up my room and making it into a game |
| **Macduff, Lennox** | **Physical Action**: To arrive at Macbeth's castle |
| | **Emotional Action**: To make sure the King is properly looked after |
| | **It Reminds Me Of**: Waking up my father when he had overslept and was supposed to be driving me to school |
| **Macbeth, Lady Macbeth** | **Physical Action**: To seem surprised and outraged at Duncan's death |
| | **Emotional Action**: To lie |
| | **It Reminds Me Of**: Pushing my clothes under my bed when my mother checked to see if I'd cleaned up my room |

(The Porter enters the courtyard by the South Gate. Loud knocking is heard.)

**PORTER:** OK, OK! I'm coming! What's the rush? No time for jokes around here. A little comedy, that's what I need. All that knocking! I know. Knock, knock! Who's there? Lettuce. Lettuce who? Let us come in or we'll break the door down! Knock, knock! Who's there? Anita. Anita who? Anita come in. Last one. Knock, knock! Who's there?

Theodore. Theodore who? Open the door! (The Porter opens the door. Macduff and Lennox enter.)

**MACDUFF:** (To the Porter) Is your master awake?

(Macbeth enters.)

We must have woken him up with our knocking. Here he comes.

(The Porter exits.)

**LENNOX:** (To Macbeth) Good morning, sir.

**MACBETH:** A good morning to you both.

**MACDUFF:** Is the King awake yet?

**MACBETH:** Not yet.

**MACDUFF:** He asked me to wake him early. Let me go to him.

**MACBETH:** No, really. Don't trouble yourself.

**MACDUFF:** He asked me. I'll go.

(Exit Macduff.)

**LENNOX:** So, the King's traveling on today?

**MACBETH:** Right. That's what he said.

**LENNOX:** It's been a terrible night. The wind made a moaning sound all night, and we could hear an owl screeching.

(Macduff enters.)

**MACDUFF:** It's horrible! I just can't believe it!

**LENNOX** and **MACBETH:** What's wrong?

**MACDUFF:** A dreadful murder!

**LENNOX:** Our King?

**MACDUFF:** Yes! Go see it for yourselves.

(Macbeth and Lennox exit.)

Wake up! Wake up, everyone! Murder! Murder!

(Lady Macbeth enters.)

**LADY MACBETH:** What's all the fuss?

(Banquo enters.)

**MACDUFF:** Oh, Banquo, Banquo! Our King has been murdered!

**LADY MACBETH:** Oh, no! In our castle?

**BANQUO:** Macduff, tell me it's not true!

(Macbeth, Lennox, and Rosse enter.)

**MACBETH:** If I had died an hour ago, I would have died a happy man.

(Malcolm and Donalbain enter.)

**DONALBAIN:** What's wrong?

**MACDUFF:** Your father has been murdered.

**MALCOLM:** Who did it?

**LENNOX:** It looks like his guards did it, but we can't punish them now. Macbeth killed them.

**MACBETH:** I saw my innocent King lying there dead, and his murderers were still there. I was furious.

**LADY MACBETH:** Oh! I feel quite faint!

**MACDUFF:** Lady Macbeth needs help.

(Lady Macbeth exits, helped by Macbeth. Everyone exits except Malcolm and Donalbain.)

**MALCOLM:** What are we going to do? Whoever killed

our father is going to try to kill us next.

**DONALBAIN:** I don't trust anyone here anymore. We'll be safer if we're apart. You go to England. I'll go to Ireland. Let's not tell anybody we're going.

(The brothers exit in opposite directions.)

# ACT THREE, Scene One

| | |
|---|---|
| **Banquo** | **Physical Action**: To honor Macbeth |
| | **Emotional Action**: To decide whether, or not, a person very important to me has done something really terrible |
| | **It Reminds Me Of**: Suspecting a friend of stealing something |
| **Macbeth, Lady Macbeth** | **Physical Action**: To receive guests in a royal way |
| | **Emotional Action**: To cover up the fact that I'm suspicious of everyone |
| | **It Reminds Me Of**: Being polite with my friends' parents but thinking that they don't really like me |
| **Murderers** | **Physical Action**: To arrive for a secret meeting with the King |
| | **Emotional Action**: To be ready for the biggest job anyone has ever asked me to do |
| | **It Reminds Me Of**: Being a ball boy for a televised, national tennis tournament |

**Rosse, Lennox**

**Physical Action**: To attend the new King's banquet

**Emotional Action**: To appear to be happy for Macbeth

**It Reminds Me Of**: Going to a

birthday party for someone I don't
really like to make another friend
happy

(The palace at Forres owned by King Macbeth of Scotland.
Banquo enters a reception hall.)

**BANQUO:** (Banquo thinks aloud.) Well, you've got it all
now, Macbeth. You've been crowned King, just like those
weird witches said. But I'm afraid you played dirty to get it.

(Macbeth enters wearing Duncan's crown, with Lennox,
Rosse, and Lady Macbeth.)

**MACBETH:** And here's our special guest! Banquo, I want
you to attend an important dinner tonight. Are you going
riding today?

**BANQUO:** Yes, I am, but if you want me at your feast, I'll
be there.

**MACBETH:** Enjoy your ride. Is your son Fleance
{FLEA-ahnts} going?

**BANQUO:** Yes.

(Banquo bows and exits.)

**MACBETH:** Now then, everyone. Your time is your own
until we dine at 7 o'clock sharp.

(Everyone exits except Macbeth.)

(Macbeth thinks aloud.) So far so good. But Banquo could
destroy me. The witches said his sons would be kings after
me. If that's true, I've risked by life for his sons. Killed
innocent Duncan for Banquo's sons. Given up my honor,
just for them. To make them kings.

(A knock is heard.)

Who's there?

(Two murderers enter.)

**MURDERER 1:** You asked us to come.

**MACBETH:** Have you thought over what I said yesterday about Banquo being the bad guy and not me?

**MURDERER 2:** We've got nothing to lose, so who cares?

**MACBETH:** But you do know that Banquo is your enemy, don't you?

**MURDERER 1:** Yeah, yeah.

**MACBETH:** You must be sure to kill Banquo and his son, Fleance. I don't want any foul-ups. Now get out of sight. Do a good job.

(All exit.)

## ACT THREE, Scene Two

| | |
|---|---|
| **Macbeth, Lady Macbeth** | **Physical Action**: To conduct a banquet |
| | **Emotional Action**: To behave in a way that will convince everyone I deserve to be King/Queen |
| | **It Reminds Me Of**: Throwing a big party and being afraid I would not be popular afterwards |
| **Rosse, Lennox, Angus, Menteith** | **Physical Action**: To attend the King's banquet |
| | **Emotional Action**: To behave as if everything is normal in the hope that normalcy will return |
| | **It Reminds Me Of**: Being at a friend's house when his parents had just had an argument |
| **Murderer 1** | **Physical Action**: To report to the King |
| | **Emotional Action**: To convince my boss that I did well even though I know I didn't |
| | **It Reminds Me Of**: Being hired to cut my neighbor's lawn and not getting it done when I promised to |
| **Ghost of Banquo** | **Physical Action**: To haunt and upset Macbeth |
| | **Emotional Action**: To get the person who wronged me to confess |

| | **It Reminds Me Of**: Staring really hard at someone who was telling a lie about me, wanting to make her feel guilty |
|---|---|

(The palace at Forres. Eight chairs are brought onstage for the banquet. Macbeth, Lady Macbeth, and several lords: Rosse, Lennox, Angus {ANG-us}, and Menteith {MEN-teeth} enter the banquet hall.)

**MACBETH:** Welcome, everyone. You know your places. Sit yourselves down.

(Lady Macbeth, Rosse, Lennox, Angus, and Menteith seat themselves.)

I would like this to be a happy occasion, a celebration of the new order in Scotland.

(Murderer 1 appears at the doorway.)

Enjoy yourselves!

(Macbeth goes to the doorway.)

You've got blood on your face.

**MURDERER 1:** It must be Banquo's. Banquo is dead. I cut his throat. But Fleance escaped, my Lord.

**MACBETH**

Oh, no! With him alive, I am still in danger. Still, he's too young to be dangerous yet. Come and see me tomorrow.

(Murderer 1 exits.)

**LADY MACBETH:** (Coming over to Macbeth) Don't leave your guests alone like this. You didn't invite them just to eat – we're supposed to be celebrating.

**MACBETH:** (To the lords) Why isn't Banquo here? It's rude and unkind of him to miss this important occasion.

**ROSSE:** Come, join us, sir.

(The ghost of Banquo enters and sits in Macbeth's place.)

**MACBETH:** (Seeing the ghost) Which one of you did this?

**ROSSE:** What do you mean, my Lord?

**LENNOX:** Gentlemen, the King is unwell.

(Lennox stands, ready to leave. Lady Macbeth goes to Macbeth.)

**LADY MACBETH:** No, no! He is sometimes like this. He's always had these strange turns, ever since he was a boy. It will pass. Don't pay any attention. (Aside to Macbeth) What are you doing now?

**MACBETH:** I'm looking at a dead man. Look! Right there! We should cut dead people into little pieces so that the parts can never make a whole ghost.

(The ghost of Banquo leaves.)

**LADY MACBETH:** Your guests are missing you, dear husband.

**MACBETH:** (To the guests) I'm sorry. I do have this strange illness. People who know me well don't worry about it. Let me sit down. (The Macbeths and Lennox sit down.) Love and health to one and all. Bring me some wine!

(A wine server enters and exits as the ghost reenters.)

I propose a toast to you, my dear friends. To our missing friend, Banquo—I wish he were here now—and to you all!

**LORDS:** To Macbeth!

(Macbeth sees the ghost.)

**MACBETH:** Go! Get out of my sight! Crawl into your grave! Your blood is cold! Your eyes are blind! Don't stare at me! (The lords stand, ready to leave.)

**LADY MACBETH:** Just think of him as slightly eccentric.

**MACBETH:** If you were alive, I'd kill you. Go, go! Get out of here!

(The ghost exits.)

Ah, that's better. More normal. Please, stay! (The lords sit down again, but they are very puzzled by Macbeth's behavior.)

**LADY MACBETH:** (To Macbeth) You've turned this night into quite a circus.

**MACBETH:** How can you look so calm when these sights make me sick with terror?

**LADY MACBETH:** He's having a bad attack. Good night. Please don't be formal. Just go. Good night to you all.

(All exit except the Macbeths.)

**MACBETH:** Why didn't Macduff come tonight? I don't trust anyone. Early tomorrow morning I'm going to find those weird witches. I want to know the worst.

**LADY MACBETH:** You need sleep.

**MACBETH:** I'm a beginner; that's my problem. It's all so new to me. Once I get used to this kind of life, I'll be fine. It's all so new to us.

(The Macbeths exit. The eight chairs are taken offstage.)

# ACT FOUR

| | |
|---|---|
| **Witches** | **Physical Action**: To toy with Macbeth |
| | **Emotional Action**: To meddle in the life of one less powerful |
| | **It Reminds Me Of**: Telling a boy and a girl what each thought about the other to see what they would do next |
| **Macbeth** | **Physical Action**: To question the witches |
| | **Emotional Action**: To get some reassurance about what's going to happen in my future |
| | **It Reminds Me Of**: Trying to get someone to give me a note that was written about me by a classmate |
| **Lennox** | **Physical Action**: To give news to the King |
| | **Emotional Action**: To make sure the most powerful person I know sees me doing my job well |
| | **It Reminds Me Of**: Carrying a message to my math teacher, whose class I find very difficult |

(Thunder is heard. Three witches enter a wild part of the Scottish woods and dance in a circle around a boiling cauldron.)

**ALL THREE WITCHES:** Hands around the cauldron go! In the poisoned entrails throw! Hubble, double, toil and trouble! Fire blaze! Macbeth is crazed!

**WITCH 1:** Scale of dragon, tooth of wolf, Blood of dog, horse's hoof, Finger of a strangled baby, Monkey's paw? No . . . well, maybe.

**ALL THREE WITCHES:** Hubble, double toil and trouble! Fire blaze! Macbeth is crazed!

**WITCH 2:** Cool it with a kitten's blood. Now the spell is sure and good.

**WITCH 3:** By the tingling in my fingers, I know that someone evil lingers.

(Macbeth enters.)

**MACBETH:** There you are! What are you doing?

**ALL THREE WITCHES:** An act without a name.

**MACBETH:** I don't care what you are doing. But answer my questions.

**WITCH 3:** Spirits will appear, and they'll answer your questions through us. Watch! . . . See? The head of an armed soldier, wearing a helmet.

**WITCH 1:** You don't have to ask anything. They read your mind. He says, "Macbeth! Macbeth! Watch out for Macduff!"

**WITCH 2:** Here's a more powerful spirit, a child covered with blood. In a tiny, childlike voice, he says, "Macbeth! You can live dangerously because no one born by a woman can harm you."

**MACBETH:** What's this! A child crowned like a king, carrying a tree?

**WITCH 3:** Don't talk! Listen! This spirit says, "Be confident, Macbeth. Be aggressive. No harm will come to you until Birnam Wood picks up and moves to Dunsinane {DUN-zeh-nane} Hill."

**MACBETH:** Well, that's not going to happen. Whoever heard of all the trees in a wood deciding to relocate? Good, this is just what I wanted to hear. But tell me one more thing. Will Banquo's son ever be King of Scotland?

**ALL THREE WITCHES:** No more! Use your eyes. Break your heart. Listen once more, then depart!

(Macbeth sees apparitions in the sky.)

**MACBETH:** Eight kings walking in a procession. And they all look like Banquo! They are his children! What a ghastly sight! You filthy hags!

(The witches disappear. Lennox enters.)

Did you see them?

**LENNOX:** Who? No. My Lord, I've come to tell you that Macduff escaped to England.

**MACBETH:** (Macbeth thinks aloud.) From now on, there's no stopping me. I shall do the very first thing that comes into my head. And I'll start by having Macduff's castle torn apart. I want his wife and children dead.

(Macbeth exits.)

# ACT FIVE, Scene One

| | |
|---|---|
| **Doctor** | **Physical Action**: To question the lady-in-waiting |
| | **Emotional Action**: To discover whether there's anything I can do to help the person who is suffering |
| | **It Reminds Me Of**: Asking my sick friend's mother how my friend was and if there was anything I could do for him |
| **Lady-in-Waiting** | **Physical Action**: To report on Lady Macbeth's condition |
| | **Emotional Action**: To help someone whose problems are really serious |
| | **It Reminds Me Of**: Talking to a family counselor before my parents' divorce |
| **Lady Macbeth** | **Physical Action**: To get my hands clean |
| | **Emotional Action**: To forget the crimes I've committed |
| | **It Reminds Me Of**: Having said something cruel on Facebook and later doing lots of mindless chores to try to keep my mind off the terrible thing I'd done |

(Macbeth's castle in Dunsinane. The doctor and the Lady-in-Waiting enter a hallway outside Lady Macbeth's bedroom.)

**DOCTOR:** When did Lady Macbeth last walk in her sleep?

**LADY-IN-WAITING:** She does it every night, sir.

**DOCTOR:** That is not normal . . . When she sleepwalks, does she speak?

**LADY-IN-WAITING:** Yes, but I don't think I should repeat what she says.

(Lady Macbeth enters, carrying a candle. She paces backward and forward and then places the candle on the floor while she rubs her hands, as if washing them.)

**DOCTOR:** How did she get that candle?

**LADY-IN-WAITING:** She always has one by her side, sir. She can't bear the darkness.

**DOCTOR:** What's she doing now? Why is she rubbing her hands together?

**LADY-IN-WAITING:** She's always doing that. Sometimes she does it for fifteen minutes at a time.

**LADY MACBETH:** Still a spot here. Come out, stain. One, two, we should be doing it now. Hell's a dark place. Shame, husband! You are a soldier, but afraid. Doesn't matter who suspects us. Who could have dreamed the old king had so much blood in him?

**DOCTOR:** Did you hear that!

**LADY MACBETH:** The Thane of Fife, he had a wife. Where is she now? Won't I ever get these hands clean? Sleep, my lord, sleep. Why can't you sleep? I can still smell blood. Oh! Wash your hands! Get ready for bed! Don't look so pale. Banquo's dead. He can't touch you now.

(Lady Macbeth picks up the candle and exits.)

**DOCTOR:** She doesn't need me. She needs God. Look after her. Any object that could harm her should be removed. Good night.

**LADY-IN-WAITING:** Thank you. Good night, Doctor.

(Lady-in-Waiting and Doctor exit in opposite directions.)

| | |
|---|---|
| **Macbeth** | **Physical Action**: To get reports of the battle |
| | **Emotional Action**: To try to keep everything from falling apart |
| | **It Reminds Me Of**: Trying to clean up after a party when my friends had made a huge mess and my parents were due home any minute |
| **Doctor** | **Physical Action**: To report on Lady Macbeth's condition |
| | **Emotional Action**: To tell a very dangerous man something he does not want to hear |
| | **It Reminds Me Of**: Telling a bully something he does not want to hear |
| **Messenger** | **Physical Action**: To report to the King |
| | **Emotional Action**: To deliver bad news without a powerful person getting angry with me |
| | **It Reminds Me Of**: Telling the principal why I was rude and disrespectful to a teacher |

(Dunsinane. Macbeth and the Doctor enter another room in the castle.)

**MACBETH:** Don't tell me any more news. I have nothing to fear until Birnam Wood moves to Dunsinane Hill. The powerful spirits who know everything said to me, "Macbeth! You can live dangerously because no one who was "born by a woman" can harm you." So you see I've got nothing to fear.

(A Messenger enters. For a moment, he can't speak.)

**MACBETH:** What's the matter? Why do you look as white as a goose?

**MESSENGER:** My Lord Macbeth! There are ten thousand . . .

**MACBETH:** Ten thousand geese?

**MESSENGER:** No, ten thousand soldiers.

**MACBETH:** Whose soldiers, you fool?

**MESSENGER:** Malcolm, Macduff, Lennox, and the English army, my Lord, They're marching this way!

**MACBETH:** I'll fight them.

(Messenger exits.)

How is your patient, Doctor?

**DOCTOR:** Not really sick, my Lord, but very disturbed by violent thoughts.

**MACBETH:** Cure her.

**DOCTOR:** The patient needs God.

**MACBETH:** Medicine isn't much help, then. Still, if you could cure my country of its ills, make Scotland healthy again, I'd applaud non-stop.

(They exit.)

## ACT FIVE, Scene Three

| | |
|---|---|
| **Malcolm, Rosse, Macduff** | **Physical Action**: To march on Macbeth's castle |
| | **Emotional Action**: To do the right thing, which I've been waiting too long to do |
| | **It Reminds Me Of**: Walking together with a large group of friends to confront a bully |

(The countryside near Birnam Wood. Malcolm, Macduff, and Rosse are marching toward Macbeth's castle.)

**MACDUFF:** What's this wood we're coming up to?

**ROSSE:** It's Birnam Wood.

**MALCOLM:** I've got an idea. I want every soldier to cut down a big branch and carry it in front of himself so that our enemy, Macbeth, won't know how many of us are coming.

(They exit.)

## ACT FIVE, Scene Four

| | |
|---|---|
| **Macbeth** | **Physical Action**: To defend the castle |
| | **Emotional Action**: To do everything I can to survive |
| | **It Reminds Me Of**: Being a captain of the basketball team and working very hard in practice to get everybody up for a game against a superior team |
| **Seyton, Messenger** | **Physical Action**: To report to the King |
| | **Emotional Action**: To deliver bad news without a powerful person getting angry with me |
| | **It Reminds Me Of**: Telling my father that, despite my best efforts, I'd got a really low grade in science |

(Macbeth's castle. Macbeth and Seyton enter.)

**MACBETH:** We have everything we need inside this castle. Bring up the drawbridge. Let them lay siege to our castle.

(A woman's scream is heard.)

What was that? Investigate that noise, Seyton {SEE-tehn}.

(Seyton exits.)

It used to make my flesh creep to hear a scream like that. But now, such horrors are quite common.

(Seyton reenters.)

**SEYTON:** The Queen is dead, my Lord.

**MACBETH:** I wish she had died when there was time to grieve properly. Life just goes on and on. The days come and go, come and go. Life's like being an actor in a play. Your worry about it, you do it, you have your moment, and then it's over. The end. All the noise and anger . . . it doesn't mean a thing.

(A Messenger enters.)

What is it?

**MESSENGER:** This is going to sound very strange, Sir, but as I was keeping watch just now, I saw Birnam Wood moving toward the castle.

**MACBETH:** If you're lying, I'll hang you from a tree. If you're not, I don't care if you hang me. I'm beginning to doubt those witches. "Be confident, Macbeth. Be aggressive. No harm will come to you until Birnam Wood picks up and moves to Dunsinane Hill." And now the Wood is approaching Dunsinane Hill. There's nothing to do but pick up our weapons and fight! Help me on with my armor!

(They exit.)

## ACT FIVE, Scene Five

| | |
|---|---|
| **Menteith, Seyton, Macbeth, Siward, Macduff** | **Physical Action**: To fight |
| | **Emotional Action**: To do everything I can to survive |
| | **It Reminds Me Of**: Playing football as hard as I could because I wanted my team to win so badly |

(Menteith and Seyton enter and fight each other. Then Macbeth and Siward enter and fight each other.)

**SIWARD:** You murderer!

(Macbeth and Siward fight. Menteith and Seyton exit, fighting. Macbeth kills Siward.)

**MACBETH:** You were born by a woman, Siward {SIGH-wehrd}.

(Macduff enters.)

Of everyone, I didn't want to meet you, Macduff. I'm already covered in your family's blood.

**MACDUFF:** What makes you think you'll win this fight?

**MACBETH:** You can't kill me. I have a charmed life. The witches said that only a man not born by a woman could kill me.

**MACDUFF:** Your charmed life is over, Macbeth. Listen to this: My mother didn't give birth to me naturally. I was removed from her by a doctor!

**MACBETH:** You can't trick me by playing with words, Macduff. I shall fight you to the death – your death!

(They exit, fighting.)

## ACT FIVE, Scene Six

| | |
|---|---|
| **Macduff** | **Physical Action**: To tell Malcolm he is now King of Scotland |
| | **Emotional Action**: To get my world back in order |
| | **It Reminds Me Of**: Counting the votes in our student council elections, hoping that the opposing sides would get along with each other after a heated campaign |
| **Malcolm** | **Physical Action**: To appear before everyone as the new King |
| | **Emotional Action**: To assure everyone that things would be all right |
| | **It Reminds Me Of**: Playing a game of soccer in which things got too competitive and then suggesting that we all get some ice cream and calm down |
| **Menteith, Lords 4-8** | **Physical Action**: To find out whether Macbeth's dead or not |
| | **Emotional Action**: To learn whether we are still at war and in danger |
| | **It Reminds Me Of**: Waiting to hear whether or not our school won the state championship |

(Malcolm, Menteith, and Lords 4, 5, 6, 7, and 8 enter and are met by Macduff, who is splattered with blood –

ketchup.)

**MACDUFF:** Welcome, my King, because that's what you are now. Macbeth is dead. We are free! Malcolm, you are the King of Scotland!

**ALL**: Long live the King!

**MALCOLM:** My only regret is that some of our dear friends had to die. Everyone who hid from Macbeth and lived in fear of him must be told that the butcher and his evil queen are dead. I thank you, one and all, and invite you to Scone, where I will be crowned King of Scotland.

(They all exit.)

# 2 RELATED NON FICTION

## NON FICTION: Macbeth and Shakespeare

A special thing about plays is the way they can make ideas come to life. William Shakespeare is the most famous playwright ever, and one of the many reasons is his ability to mix pieces of existing stories with names from history to make vivid and memorable plots of his own.

Shakespeare read about the story of Macbeth in a book called Holinshed's Chronicles, a popular history of Britain published when Shakespeare was 13. The real Macbeth had died more than 500 years before Shakespeare was born. A modern American would have to be writing about a time before Columbus to find a story that old. The story in Holinshed is a lot like the story Shakespeare uses for his play, which he wrote at age 42 when he was near the end of his career.

The story is about a general, Macbeth, who is a hero in battle. He is honored by the king. Then he meets three apparently magical creatures, the "weird sisters," who start making predictions that come true. Then, they assure Macbeth that no harm can come to him, no matter what he does. Macbeth's wife wants to be queen and urges Macbeth to murder the king. They go through with the crime.

The play takes this grim story from Holinshed and flies with it into a higher atmosphere. We realize we are looking at a huge story about the lies we can tell ourselves when we do things we know are wrong. We see a story of what is called hubris, which is a word that means you think you're too good for everybody, too important to have to play by the rules. We see a cosmic story that asks whether we even really have choices and free will: Is that just an illusion created by a perversity that somehow rules the universe?

These powerful themes of ambition and fate, the incredible language of the original play, which we hope you will read after you've worked on this adaptation, and the powerful emotions shown in the play, not only bring history to life, they bring issues in your own time into a new framework, one built by the greatest playwright of them all.


## NON FICTION: Banquo and Probability

Banquo says the witches' prediction that Macbeth would be Thane of Cawdor is simply a "coincidence." A coincidence is something that might seem to be connected to another event, but most likely, it's just random luck.

Today, luck, or chance, is understood in great detail with math. The concept of probability - how likely it is that something will happen - is given a number value. A value of 0 (zero) means something absolutely will not happen and a value of 1 means something absolutely will happen. So, in the real world, probability is always a fraction. If you toss a coin, there is a 0.5 chance of the coin landing heads-up. The actual numbers you experience flipping coins will tend to approach half-and-half the more times you flip.

The mathematical understanding of probability came after Shakespeare's time. In the 1560s, Gerolamo Cardano, an Italian, tried to calculate the math of throwing dice. It is not likely that Shakespeare knew about Cardano. It wasn't until the 1660s, about 50 years after Shakespeare died, that Blaise Pascal and Pierre de Fermat, two French math geniuses, really developed the math of probability in letters they wrote to each other.

So, when Shakespeare wrote Macbeth, two events that seemed connected were very likely to be thought of as really connected, even if that connection had to be through magic. This would have been even more likely in the year 1055, when the real Macbeth lived, more than 500 years before Shakespeare.


## NON FICTION: Witches and King James

The Macbeth story in Holinshed's Chronicles does not use the word witch. Shakespeare choose to call these characters witches.

What's a witch? Today we think of witches as creatures in stories in which magical things happen. The term can also mean a follower of certain kinds of beliefs and rituals. Among those is a sort of nature worship that dates back probably thousands of years.

King James the Sixth of Scotland was afraid of what he believed were the powers of witches. He even thought they could cause storms to sink ships at sea. He published a book called Daemonologie in 1597. Shakespeare drew a lot of ideas from this book when writing Macbeth.

James became King James the First of England in 1603, upon the death of Queen Elizabeth the First. Being a witch was against the law, and many people were executed by the government for supposedly being witches. Campaigns to arrest witches were called "witch-hunts." They continued in England for 100 years. The anti-witchcraft law in England was not repealed until 1951, though it had not been enforced for generations.

## NON FICTION: King James and the Gunpowder Plot

Not everybody liked King James. On the night between the 4th and 5th of November, 1605, a Catholic named Guy Fawkes was caught in a basement of Parliament. That's the main government building in London, England. King James and his family were going to be there the morning of the 5th. All the government leaders were going to be there.

Guy Fawkes was caught with enough gunpowder to blow up the building. he was arrested, tried, and ultimately executed.

This became known as the Gunpowder Plot.

The destruction of Parliament was planned as the start of a Catholic revolution. The failure of the Gunpowder Plot left the Protestant power structure strong.

Guy Fawkes Day is celebrated in England. People set off fireworks every November 5th. They often burn a dummy called a "Guy."

It is believed that Shakespeare's writing of Macbeth was influenced by this event, by other plots against King James, and by James's interest in witchcraft.

## NON FICTION: Skara Brae and Edinburgh Castle

We sometimes think of countries as permanent, but they change. Scotland - Alba in the Scottish Gaelic language - is ancient. This picture shows a place called Skara Brae, where people have lived for 6,000 years. These stone dwellings are on the mainland of the Orkney Islands. The Orkneys are about 70 islands that are part of Scotland. Scotland has nearly 800 islands.

Below is a picture of Edinburgh castle. It is in the capital city of Scotland, Edinburgh (pronounced "ED-in-burr-uh").

People have lived on that hill for at least 11,000 years. The oldest part of the castle is St. Margaret's chapel, pictured as an inset. It dates from the 12th century. Robert the Bruce, who led the fight for Scottish independence from England, destroyed all the other castle buildings that were standing at that time in a battle in 1314.

## NON FICTION: Comic Relief

The Porter scene in Macbeth is one of the most famous examples in all of literature of something called "comic relief." In dramatic stories, writers like to put something funny. It gives the audience or reader "relief" from the dramatic tension.

In many movies today, heroes have funny things to say even when the situation they are in is very dangerous. That is one kind of comic relief. It makes the hero seem even cooler for being able to joke despite the danger.

Another form of comic relief is a funny sidekick - somebody who isn't the main hero but who is on the hero's side.

Shakespeare's play Hamlet is very serious, but it has a scene with two gravediggers who say silly things. This is comic relief.

A modern famous musical play called Les Miserables is very serious, but it has a song called "Master of the House" which is very funny.

The next time you write a serious story, try putting something funny in there as well. See how it works!

## NON FICTION: Refrigeration and the Wasted Feast

With Banquo's Ghost ending the night early, this feast would have been a huge waste.

In medieval times, the poor ate very simply. Rough bread, sometimes with pea or bean flour mixed in, plus some cheese and a bowl of curds, would have been a day's diet. The servants in big houses more regularly had meat, better bread, and pudding, among other things. Merchants, minor lords - in positions like Macbeth's at the start of the play - would have a lot of different foods and drink brought out all at once or as things were cooked.

There is a history-of-science reason that a king's feast helped feed the servants better than other people at the time, and that Macbeth's feast would have been a huge waste. Refrigeration. Or, lack of refrigeration. No place to plug your refrigerator in back in the year 1055. Not in Shakespeare's time, either.

Without being able to keep meat cold, the old way to preserve it was with salt. Salt was rare and expensive. It was cheaper to eat a whole goat, for example, than to try to save leftovers. So, sending all those guests home without dinner in the play does not mean that the Macbeth's can enjoy re-heated lunches for the next three weeks.

Maybe you could write a play about the servants sneaking the extra food out of the palace at Forres and feeding the poor in the village!


## NONFICTION: The Curse of Macbeth

There was a widespread belief in ghosts in Shakespeare's time, and ghost stories are still very popular today. Generally, people think of two kinds of ghosts - the ghost of a dead person or a kind of evil spirit or demon.

In Shakespeare's play Hamlet, the ghost of a dead king talks to his son, Hamlet. He is a popular type of ghost - angry because he was murdered. The Ghost of Banquo doesn't speak in Macbeth. You could write this scene differently, adding lines for the Ghost of Banquo.

Macbeth, the play itself, is supposed to have a curse. A curse is a sort of magical spell. The curse of Macbeth is a rule that you must not say the name of the play while in a theater. If you do, according to the curse, terrible things will happen. If you say the word Macbeth by accident, you can go through a process that is supposed to stop the curse from happening. You must go outside the theater, spin around three times, spit, say a bad word, and then knock and ask to be allowed back inside.

How Macbeth got this curse is not known. Some say that Shakespeare used real witches' spells in the script and so witches cursed the play.
The curse of Macbeth is not the only superstition in the theater world. Maybe the other best-known belief is that it's bad luck to wish theater people "good luck." Instead, people say, "break a leg." This phrase has two meanings, and one is an obvious paradox: It's a way of wishing a person really bad luck as a way of wishing them good luck.

The other meaning of "break a leg" comes from another meaning of the word "leg." In many theaters, there are curtains not only in front of the stage, but also along the sides. Those hanging curtains on the sides are called "legs." So to "break a leg" is to enter onto the stage through one of those side curtains.

One of the most interesting theater superstitions is that it's bad luck to whistle in a theater, unless it's in the script. This may have started as a practical rule, however. People who worked on theatrical rigging - the ropes and weights that hold up the curtains, backdrops, and other things - came from ships' crews. They were accustomed to rigging sails. Ships' crews used whistles as commands. So, a random whistle in a theater might make a crew member do something dangerous, thinking the whistle is a command, for example, to drop the sails.

## NONFICTION: Staging Hallucinations

Hallucination is seeing or hearing something that isn't really there. Showing a hallucination on stage is very dramatic. Macbeth sees a dagger that isn't really there the night he kills Duncan. He sees Banquo's Ghost. Finally, he sees these strange visions while the witches make promises to him.

Most people who stage the play don't make a real dagger float in the air. Usually, there is an actor who plays Banquo's Ghost. The apparitions in Act Four can be staged in many different ways, or not seen at all by the audience.

These kinds of decisions about how to put on a play are called choices, usually made by the director in the modern theater. In Shakespeare's time, the writer and one or more main actors made these kinds of choices.

Think about the real world challenge of these three hallucinations: the dagger, the Ghost, and the apparitions. How would you show each one on stage? Why might some ways of showing these hallucinations work better than other ways? Why might you choose not to show anything, but rather to let the words paint the picture in the audience's mind?

Now discuss how you might show these hallucinations if you were making a movie and could use computer-generated special effects.

# NONFICTION: Macbeth and Mental Illness

The Doctor says that the queen's problem is not something he can treat - that she needs God, not a doctor. The Doctor and Lady-in-Waiting might suspect that Lady Macbeth is guilty. The things she talks about are clues that she might have had a part in King Duncan's murder. The Doctor may be saying that Lady Macbeth's problem is not sickness, but sin.

We, a modern audience, tend to think about Lady Macbeth's behavior in a different way. We try to understand her situation through psychology.

Psyche (SIGH-key) is the Greek word for mind. Psychology is the study of the human mind. However, it was not until more than 250 years after Shakespeare that this study became separate from general philosophy. Experts gradually have come to study the human mind more and more scientifically. Today, 400 years after Shakespeare, our understanding of the human mind has a lot to do with biology and chemistry. Today, a doctor would not deny that Lady Macbeth is sick - with a mental illness.

Modern people would generally say that Lady Macbeth is mentally ill from the beginning of the play. She doesn't seem to care about people's feelings or even their lives. She worries that Macbeth is too nice to kill Duncan - which sounds very sick to the modern ear.

You might want to look up the words schizophrenia and sociopath to get started thinking and writing about Lady Macbeth from a modern psychological perspective.

A famous literature expert named Harold Bloom wrote a book called Shakespeare: The Invention of the Human. Bloom's idea is that Shakespeare did more than simply studying human nature in his writing, that in fact Shakespeare was so powerful that he actually helped shape what it means to be human through the invention of characters like the Macbeths, Hamlet, Othello, and King Lear.

Does that sound possible to you? Can a writer create something so powerful that it goes beyond reporting and showing what people are like, and actually causes the human race to change?

Well, recently, a new mental illness has been unofficially named the Truman Show Delusion, or TSD. The Truman Show was a 1998 fictional movie about a person whose entire life is shown on TV as a reality show, using hidden cameras. The movie came before reality TV shows became so very popular. People suffering from TSD believe that they are living their lives entirely on camera. They talk to themselves, thinking that they're talking to an audience of millions of TV viewers.

Think about that! Before the Truman Show and before reality-TV, it would have been very unlikely for a person suffering from mental illness to imagine that he or she was being watched on TV all the time. Such people used to think they were being watched by spies or spirits, or that they were some kind of royalty, or even an alien.

In other words, the real environment in which people find themselves can have an effect on their mental state. Therefore, mental illness isn't always the same from decade to decade, century to century, and what we consider a normally functioning human mind may also change over time.

## NONFICTION: C- Section

The birth procedure described by Macduff is known as a Caesarean section, or C-section.

A "section," in medicine, means a separation by cutting.

The legend that gives this operation its name is that the Roman ruler Julius Caesar was born this way. This seems not to be true. Caesar's mother lived 46 years after giving birth to Julius, and there are no reliable reports of women surviving a C-section for more than 1,000 years after that time. In 100 BC, when Caesar was born, the operation was only used when women were dying or had died trying to give birth.

# 3 PLOT

The plot is the sequence of events that take place in a play. Understanding the plot is essential to both actors and audiences. Here are some questions about the plot of Macbeth.

1. What does King Duncan give to Macbeth?

2. What two titles do the witches predict Macbeth will have?

3. What does Lady Macbeth want?

4. What are Macbeth's reasons for resisting the plan to murder Duncan?

5. Describe Lady Macbeth's plan to kill Duncan.

6. Immediately after the murder, Lady Macbeth and Macbeth have very different states of mind. Describe them.

7. How does Macbeth explain the guards' deaths?

8. Who are Malcolm and Donalbain? What do they do upon learning that Duncan is dead?

9. What does Macbeth hire the two murderers to do?

10. What are the two riddles that trick Macbeth into thinking he is safe?

11. Who attacks Macbeth's castle?

12. Describe how the riddle concerning Birnam Wood

comes true.

13. Why is Macduff able to kill Macbeth?

14. Who succeeds Macbeth to the throne of Scotland?

15. Where will the coronation take place?

# 4 VOCABULARY

GAME: In a circle, or group, each person talks about the play using the next word in the list. Add your own words and make your own lists. Small groups can play simultaneously. One group might perform a conversation about the play for the whole class.

battlefield
friends
rivalry
predict
startled
traitor
ambitious
cautious
confused
celebration
encouraged
manipulate
murder
deranged
eccentric
innocent
predicted
rebellious
supernatural
traitor
weird

# 5 READING ACTIVITIES

1. Read the script aloud in class. The teacher may give coaching so that students read with purpose and understanding.

2. Do a **dramatic reading**. Actors sit on chairs in a semicircle reading from their scripts. One person introduces the lay's setting and reads the stage directions aloud, sitting some distance apart from the actors so that the audience doesn't get confused. Rehearsals and performance should take about 5 classroom periods.

3. Do a **staged reading**. Actors move on a stage while reading their parts form the script. It is not a polished performance; rather, it is designed to let the actors get the physical feel of the play. Rehearsals and performance should take about 10 classroom periods.

4. **Narrated scenes and dramatic excerpts** is an experimental way of presenting Macbeth that provides opportunities for narrative writing. Select several crucial scenes to be fully staged. Assign narrators to tell the audience what happened before or after these scenes. The students will have to turn the play's dialogue into third-person prose. Rehearsals and performance should take about 15 periods.

5. **CONTEXT GAME**: One student chooses and reads a speech from the adaptation or from the original in front of the class. Then, he or she asks "Who said that?" The student who gives the correct answer is the next one to choose and read a speech. A more advanced version of the game might insist on students naming the Act and Scene the speech came from and a description of that scene.

# 6 WRITING ACTIVITIES

1 Write an opinion piece: Macbeth was a Good Man Destroyed by Ambition

2 Write an opinion piece: Studying Macbeth teaches the reader not to be superstitious.

3 Research the Gunpowder Plot. How is it relevant to this play?

4 Research what the Elizabethans believed about magic and the supernatural world.

5 Research the role of weather in this play. Search the original play for weather references.

6 Explain how Macbeth grew so confident that no one could hurt him.

7 Write a scene as a series of text messages.

8 Transpose a scene from script format to prose. Use quotation marks and add narrative description.

9 Imagine you are Lady Macbeth. Write a blog to describe your activities and thoughts.

10 Write Tweets from Macbeth to Lady Macbeth.

11 Write Tweets between the Witches.

12 Write an obituary for Macbeth.

13 Rewrite the story of Macbeth where everyone has a smart phone.

# 7 DISCUSSIONS

1 Why do you think Shakespeare started the play with the Witches?

2 What looks good that is actually bad?

3 When is ambition a good thing?

4 What does Lady Macbeth mean when she says, "I shall have to forget I am a woman for a while"?

5 Describe the differences between Macbeth and Lady Macbeth.

6 Did Macbeth imagine the Witches and the dagger?

7 What makes Macbeth such a tragic character?

8 Do Macbeth and Lady Macbeth have a good marriage?

9 Would you call Macbeth brave?

10 Compare Lady Macbeth's and Macbeth's behavior at the feast.

11 Do you feel sorry for Macbeth?

12 What do the Witches do?

13 Why does Lady Macbeth hate the darkness?

14 What is guilt?

15 The Witches spoke in riddles. What is a riddle?

**16 What do you think Shakespeare wanted the audience of Macbeth to learn?**

# 8 EVALUATION

1 When was the original Macbeth written and by whom?
2 In what country does Macbeth take place?
3 Did a man or woman originally play Lady Macbeth?
4 Give two examples of supernatural elements in the play.
5 Explain what the Witches mean when they say to Banquo, "Less than Macbeth, but more."
6 In Act One, the Witches chant, "good looks bad and bad looks good." Give two examples from the play of someone bad seeming to be good.
7 Give two reasons why Macbeth hesitates to murder Duncan.
8 How many Acts are there in Macbeth?
9 What do the Witches predict for Banquo?
10 How does Birnam Wood move to Dunsinane Hill?

# 9 SELF-EVALUATION

Doing a drama project involves using all the skills, common sense, and concentration you have. Helping someone learn lines or researching and making costumes for a scene have probably helped you discover interests and skills that you didn't know you had. Perhaps you also discovered  areas in which you need to improve? Think about this experience. Think about your own behavior during this Macbeth project. When you were having fun and the work seemed easy, you were probably good at the activity. When the word was hard, what was it that made it difficult? Assess your own strengths, needs, and goals.

1 Studying Macbeth has made me realize that I am good at the following:

2 Studying Macbeth has shown me that I need to work on the following:

3 This drama project has allowed me to learn about myself and what I think about the world. Here is what I learned:

# 10 CONNECT WITH OTHERS

Having a real audience for your work is exciting and teaches you so much. Please reach out and create a real audience for your work on Macbeth. Here are some suggestions:

1 Do a live dramatic reading for, or with, another class.
2 Memorize and record a scene. Post the video on your classroom website and ask students and parents for feedback.
3 Look at videos that other students have posted about Macbeth on YouTube. As a class, discuss the work and then make constructive, online comments.
4 Email the author of this adaptation and describe your work: Annabelle@BigFunEducation.org
5 Join some Google Communities and arrange to "Hangout" with other students studying Macbeth. Join the Google Plus Community called Big Fun PLAYS: https://plus.google.com/u/0/communities/1065398435 36943892726
6 You might like to do a Mystery Hangout with students living in Scotland. Join our Mystery Hangout Community on Google Plus and discover a Scottish class: https://plus.google.com/u/0/communities/1103691201 41935358658
7 You can also follow our Big Fun Education page on Google Plus to find out what we are working on: https://plus.google.com/u/0/b/10189093360759226050 3/+BigfuneducationOrgK-12/posts

8 We did a project called Macbeth Goes Social with 400 students around the world. Check out how we did it here:

https://www.youtube.com/watch?v=83FSZueirHo&feature=share&list=PLfDezy4NAbiZC_ZHe_7-PkewVAm6nJchS&index=7

9 We have 46 YouTubes recording what we did to connect 400 students studying Macbeth around the world. You can see them here:

https://www.youtube.com/playlist?list=PLfDezy4NAbiZC_ZHe_7-PkewVAm6nJchS

10 Watch our YouTube called "A Feast In The Castle" where 3 classes learn about cooking for the Macbeths. We had a dramaturg from the Yale School of Drama join two chefs (UK and Trinidad), and three classes from USA, UK, and Argentina. Lots of FUN!

https://www.youtube.com/watch?v=ZzdBEG33Qr4&list=PLfDezy4NAbiZC_ZHe_7-PkewVAm6nJchS&index=26

11 Subscribe to our YouTube Channel and connect:

https://www.youtube.com/channel/UCV6TwdIz-wbmvOkrks_UlHQ/videos

# ABOUT THE SERIES

Grants from **Google, The Dudley T. Dougherty Foundation, People's United Community Foundation,** and the **Frances R. Dewing Foundation** have allowed the nonprofit, BIG FUN education, to create **Big Fun PLAYS for K-12.** Students listen to an audio play while following an illustrated script on screen. Related nonfiction pieces, acting exercises, and discussion prompts are embedded in the scripts. 40 academic words are targeted in each play and have clickable explanations. We motivate and scaffold students towards cross-curricular knowledge and bring the text exemplars in Appendix B of the CCS to life. www.BigFunEducation.org This series of paperback books for schools helps us offer the online plays for free.

Printed in Great Britain
by Amazon